JOHN McMANUS

p.112 - the illegal trial of Jesus

A Study of the Gospel of Mark

A Study of
The Gospel of Mark

HUGH R. PETERSON

Convention Press

NASHVILLE   TENNESSEE

© 1958 · CONVENTION PRESS
Nashville, Tennessee

All rights reserved
International copyright secured

531-00023

Library of Congress Catalog Card Number: 58-10534
Printed in the United States of America
300. AL 58 R.R.D.

About the Author

HUGH R. PETERSON was born in Gore, New Zealand, November 21, 1903, and spent several years in the service of the Bank of Australasia there. He came to the United States in 1926 for his formal education and is now a naturalized citizen.

Dr. Peterson received the B.A. degree from Georgetown College. While a student there he served as a Baptist Student Union worker and as associate pastor of the Georgetown Baptist Church. He received the Th.B., Th.M., and Ph.D. degrees from the Southern Baptist Theological Seminary, Louisville, Kentucky, where he served as fellow in the Department of Church Administration. He holds an honorary doctorate from Georgetown College.

Since 1937, Dr. Peterson has been on the staff of the Southern Baptist Theological Seminary, serving successively as student counselor, registrar, dean of students, director of admissions, secretary of the faculties and, presently, dean of administration. He has served as the pastor of the Mill Creek Baptist Church, near Bardstown, Kentucky; and, for ten years, the Sonora Baptist Church, Sonora, Kentucky; and has been the interim pastor of eleven churches in the Louisville area.

Dr. Peterson's writing assignments have included Adult and Young People's Sunday school lessons; Young People's Training Union programs; the "Altar Fires" section of *Home Life* magazine; and *Open Windows.* He has periodically conducted the Sunday school hour on one of the Louisville radio stations.

Dr. Peterson is married to the daughter of a Baptist preacher. They have one teen-age son, Hugh, Jr.

Sunday School Training Course

THE Sunday School Training Course prepared by the Sunday School Department of the Baptist Sunday School Board is one of the major means of promoting Sunday school work. Its influence is limited only by its use.

The six sections of the course include studies in Bible, doctrines, evangelism, Sunday school leadership and administration, teaching, age group studies, and special studies. The range of the course is broad, for the field of Sunday school work is broad and requires comprehensive and specific training. Sixteen books are required for the completion of each diploma.

The study of the Training Course is not to be limited to the present Sunday school workers. Most churches need twice as many workers as are now enlisted. This need can be supplied by training additional workers now. Members of the Young People's and Adult classes and older Intermediates should be led to study these books, for thereby will their service be assured. Parents will find help as they study what the Sunday school is trying to do.

Special Note to Instructor

During your teaching of this book, will you check with the Sunday school superintendent and see if an accurate record of training for the workers is kept. If not, please urge him to set up such a file, with an associate superintendent of training in charge. Filing materials—cards, envelopes, or loose-leaf sheets—may be ordered at nominal cost from your nearest Baptist Book Store.

A. V. WASHBURN
Secretary, Sunday School Department
Baptist Sunday School Board

Contents

Some Projected Visual Materials viii

Introduction ix

1. INSIGHTS INTO THE FIRST OF THE GOSPELS 3

2. THE BEGINNING OF THE GOSPEL 17

3. THE GREAT GALILEAN MINISTRY 33

4. WITHDRAWING FROM GALILEE 51

5. MOVING TOWARD JERUSALEM 67

6. LAST PUBLIC MINISTRY IN JERUSALEM 85

7. FINAL HOURS WITH THE DISCIPLES 101

8. THE ARREST, TRIAL, AND CRUCIFIXION OF JESUS . . . 117

9. THE RISEN LORD 133

Questions for Review and Examination 147

Directions for the Teaching and Study of This Book for Credit 149

Some Projected Visual Materials

For Use in Teaching This Book

THE CLASS PERIODS should primarily be devoted to study of the Scripture passages—with a Bible in the hands of each class member. For use during the assembly period, and (to a limited extent) as supplementary material for the class periods, selections may be made from the following list:

CHAPTER 2—Filmstrip: *The Ministry of John the Baptist.* Motion pictures: *Message of John the Baptist; Jesus and the Fishermen*

CHAPTER 3—Filmstrips: *Jesus' First Tour of Galilee; Jesus at a Festival in Jerusalem; Jesus' Second Tour of Galilee.* Motion pictures: *Thy Sins Are Forgiven; Jesus, Lord of Sabbath; Jesus and the Lepers; I Am the Resurrection*

CHAPTER 4—Filmstrips: *Jesus Withdraws from Galilee; Jesus Teaches Humility and Forgiveness*

CHAPTER 6—Motion picture: *Last Journey to Jerusalem*

CHAPTER 7—Filmstrip: *The Last Supper.* Motion pictures: *The Upper Room; Betrayal in Gethsemane*

CHAPTER 8—*The Crucifixion.* Motion pictures: *Jesus Before the High Priest; Trial Before Pilate; The Crucifixion*

CHAPTER 9—Filmstrips: *Jesus' Resurrection; Jesus' Later Appearances.* Motion picture: *The Lord Is Risen*

A number of slides depict scenes from the Gospel of Mark. *Focus,* the audio-visual aids catalogue, lists the slides by number and title and indicates the Scripture passage which each slide illustrates. It also gives descriptions and prices of the motion pictures and filmstrips.

Introduction

THE STORY OF the earthly ministry of our Lord and Saviour Jesus Christ is the fountainhead of our Christian faith. The crisp, clear style of Mark's Gospel makes the study of the life and work of Jesus a sheer delight as well as a source of spiritual inspiration and instruction. The fact that Mark presents this story in chronological order more than do any of the other three Gospel writers enables the reader to follow the ministry of Jesus step by step and to walk again where Jesus walked.

Reference has been made in this book to the other Gospel accounts of the life of Jesus only when Mark summarizes some incident or when the other writers add some significant and relevant statement to Mark's record. However, the reader would do well to keep a harmony of the Gospels handy in order to get an over-all view of the life and ministry of Jesus.

In view of the limitations of space, no attempt has been made, for the most part, to give an extensive interpretation of specific passages in Mark's Gospel. The primary purpose of the book is to assist the reader in outlining the Gospel so that its content may be better understood and more clearly kept in mind.

It is impossible to acknowledge all of the help that has been received from other writers in the preparation of this book. The author has found two recent volumes especially helpful and genuinely stimulating: *The Gospel of Mark* by William Barclay of Trinity College, Glasgow; and *The Gospel According to Mark* by Ernest Trice Thompson, of Union Theological Seminary, Richmond, Virginia.

The author wishes to express appreciation to A. V. Washburn of the Baptist Sunday School Board of the Southern

Baptist Convention for the invitation to prepare this book; to J. Estill Jones, associate professor of New Testament Interpretation at the Southern Baptist Theological Seminary; and William J. Fallis, book editor of the Baptist Sunday School Board, for helpful suggestions in the preparation of the manuscript; and to the publishers of the works cited for permission to use these materials from their publications.

It is the sincere prayer of the writer that this book may be used by the Holy Spirit to give those who study it a fuller understanding of the life and ministry of our Lord Jesus Christ and a new appreciation of the fact that he is, indeed, "the author and finisher of our faith" (Heb. 12:2).

HUGH R. PETERSON

A Study of the Gospel of Mark

CHAPTER 1

I. THE AUTHOR OF THE FIRST OF THE GOSPELS
   1. Son of Mary Who Lived in Jerusalem
   2. Companion of Paul and Barnabas
   3. With Paul in Rome
   4. With Peter in Rome

II. WHY MARK WROTE HIS GOSPEL
   1. Led by the Holy Spirit
   2. Need for a Written Record
   3. Strength and Comfort for Persecuted Christians
   4. The Mighty Works of Jesus

III. THE PLAN OF MARK'S GOSPEL
   1. An Introduction (1:1–20)
   2. The Great Galilean Ministry (1:21 to 6:13)
   3. Ministry in Areas Outside of Galilee (6:14 to 10:52)
   4. Final Ministry in Jerusalem (11:1 to 14:42)
   5. The Crucifixion and Resurrection (14:43 to 16:20)

IV. THE CHARACTERISTICS OF MARK'S GOSPEL
   1. The Simple Story of Jesus
   2. Written for Gentile Believers
   3. The Deity of Jesus
   4. The Humanity of Jesus

1

INSIGHTS INTO THE FIRST OF THE GOSPELS

THROUGH all the ages mankind longed for a more intimate knowledge of God. In the fulness of time, God answered this universal longing by sending his Son into the world, "who being the brightness of his glory, and the express image of his person, and upholding all things by the word of his power, when he had by himself purged our sins, sat down on the right hand of the Majesty on high" (Heb. 1:3). This story of God's revelation of himself in human form has been recorded in the Four Gospels.

Each of the Gospel writers tells his story from a slightly different point of view and with a different purpose in mind. Matthew, writing with Jewish believers in mind, presents Jesus as the promised Messiah and indicates, over and over again, how the Scriptures were fulfilled in his life and ministry. Luke, who wrote for Gentile believers, emphasizes the universal saviourhood of Jesus. John wrote in a day when men were questioning the eternal existence of Jesus, so he presents Jesus as the eternal Christ. Mark is primarily concerned with the activity of Jesus upon the earth as he introduced the kingdom of God among men.

Though the precise date on which each of these books was written is not known, it is fairly certain that Mark's Gospel was the first of them. Evidence for this assertion is found partly in the fact that all but some twenty verses in

Mark's Gospel are included in either Matthew or Luke. It is assumed that Mark's Gospel had been in circulation long enough to have come to the attention of the other two Gospel writers before they wrote their manuscripts. John's Gospel was quite evidently written at a still later date. Some scholars have placed the date of the writing of Mark's Gospel between A.D. 55–60. Others place it somewhere between A.D. 65–70—shortly after the death of both Paul and Peter and shortly before the fall of Jerusalem.

I. THE AUTHOR OF THE FIRST OF THE GOSPELS

As you read the Four Gospels, you will notice that in no case is the name of the writer clearly indicated in the text of the book. In the book attributed to him, John makes certain references to "the disciple whom Jesus loved" and to "the other disciple," which seem to indicate that the book came from his pen. Luke gives us a clue to the authorship of the Third Gospel as he begins the Acts of the Apostles, which he most certainly wrote (see Acts 1:1). But there is no such clue to the author's identity in the Gospel of Mark. Early Christian tradition, however, claimed that Mark was its author.

The only person of that name who was intimately connected with the New Testament story was John Mark, who is mentioned several times in the book of Acts (12:12; 12:25; 15:37–39), and in the writings of Paul (Col. 4:10; 2 Tim. 4:11; Philemon 24), and once in the First Epistle of Peter (1 Peter 5:13).

1. *Son of Mary Who Lived in Jerusalem*

From the references cited, it would appear that the writer of the first of the Gospels was John Mark, who lived with his mother Mary, in Jerusalem. It was in their house that the disciples met to pray for the release of Peter from prison.

It was to this house that Peter went after his miraculous deliverance by the angel of the Lord.

It is supposed by some Bible scholars that the upper room where Jesus observed the Passover meal with his disciples on the eve of his crucifixion was also in the house of Mary, the mother of Mark, and that it was in this house that the disciples gathered after our Lord's ascension into heaven. All of these circumstances would mean that Mark was in close contact with the immediate followers of Jesus in his youth. Many of the stories of Jesus that the Gospel writer tells so simply, but in such minute detail, he no doubt first heard from the lips of the apostles.

2. *Companion of Paul and Barnabas*

When Barnabas and Paul left Jerusalem to take up residence at Antioch, they "took with them John, whose surname was Mark" (Acts 12:25). When the Holy Spirit said to the Christians at Antioch, "Separate me Barnabas and Saul for the work whereunto I have called them" (Acts 13:2), these first two Christian missionaries agreed to make the young man, Mark, their traveling companion. It was an unhappy experience for Mark. When the company arrived at Perga in Pamphylia (Acts 13:13), Mark evidently decided that he had had enough and returned to Jerusalem.

Paul was quite disappointed in the young man and, when plans were being made for the second missionary journey, Paul steadfastly refused to give Mark another chance. "And the contention was so sharp between them [Barnabas and Paul], that they departed asunder one from the other: and so Barnabas took Mark, and sailed unto Cyprus" (Acts 15:39). Mark's acquaintanceship with Paul, at that time, was short-lived. Mark was with Paul long enough, however, to hear a great deal about Jesus as Paul had come to learn about Jesus in his own experience and in his conversations with the apostles upon his first visit to Jerusalem after his conversion.

3. *With Paul in Rome*

The estrangement between Paul and Mark eventually came to an end. When Paul wrote his epistle to the Colossians, probably about A.D. 62, Mark was with him in Rome. Paul was apparently concerned that the Colossians might hold against Mark his previous unfaithfulness to the cause. He urged them to receive Mark, to take him to their hearts, as it were (Col. 4:10). In the letter to Philemon (v. 24 ASV) written from Rome at the same time, Paul honors Mark with the title "fellow-worker." Paul's genuine affection for Mark is evident in his word to Timothy as he wrote: "Take Mark, and bring him with thee: for he is profitable to me for the ministry" (2 Tim. 4:11).

In his attitude toward Mark, near the end of his life, Paul had caught the spirit of Jesus who taught forgiveness. Paul had decided that it was not good to hold one grievous mistake against a man for the rest of his days. He was quite willing to give the young man a chance to prove himself, and Mark had gladly seized the opportunity to make good.

4. *With Peter in Rome*

Mark learned many of the facts concerning Jesus that he would include in his Gospel, from Paul and from the disciples in Jerusalem and, indeed, from Barnabas as they labored together in Cyprus. It is believed that Mark was perhaps still more influenced and instructed by the apostle Peter, possibly in Rome (see 1 Peter 5:13). The relationship between Peter and Mark was quite close. Peter's brief reference to Mark as his "son" has led many to believe that Mark owed his conversion to the apostle Peter.

During the year or more that Peter and Mark were so closely associated, they must have engaged in many earnest conversations about their Lord, whom both loved so dearly and whom Peter knew so well. Papias, one of the outstanding Christian writers of the second century, went so far as to say that much of Mark's Gospel is a reproduction of the sermons which Peter preached in his last days in Rome. Papias claims to have received this information from the apostle John, whom he knew personally. Here is what Papias wrote, in about the year A.D. 140, as quoted by the noted church historian, Eusebius:

> This also the presbyter (John) used to say: Mark, indeed, who became the interpreter of Peter, wrote accurately, as far as he remembered them, the things said or done by the Lord, but not in order. For he (Mark) had neither heard the Lord nor been his personal follower, but at a later stage, as I said, he had followed Peter, who used to adapt his teachings to the needs of the moment, but not as though he were drawing up a connected account of the oracles of our Lord: so that Mark committed no error in writing certain matters just as he remembered them. For he had only one object in view, namely, to leave out nothing of the things which he had heard, and to include no false statement among them.[1]

To those of us who have sometimes wondered why Peter never wrote the story of Jesus, this testimony gives a possible answer. In some sense at least, the Gospel of Mark is the story of Jesus according to Peter, as preserved by Mark, under the leadership of the Holy Spirit. In a sense it is the story of an eyewitness, since Mark saw Jesus through the eyes of one of our Lord's closest disciples.

II. Why Mark Wrote His Gospel

The meaning of Mark's Gospel can best be understood as we bear in mind the purposes for which it was written.

1. *Led by the Holy Spirit*

Uppermost in Mark's mind, surely, was the conviction that he was led by the Holy Spirit to produce a dependable and authentic written record of the life and work of his Lord for the edification and instruction of the Christians of his day and especially, perhaps, for the Christians in and around the city of Rome. Mark had no way of knowing that his story would be preserved through the ages, by the providence of God, as a part of the sacred Scriptures. Nevertheless, he must have had the conviction born in his heart by the Holy Spirit that his words would reveal the truth about Jesus Christ to those who read them and would thus lead them into a knowledge of Christ as Saviour and Lord.

2. *Need for a Written Record*

Mark not only felt the leadership of the Spirit; he also sensed the real need for a written record of the earthly ministry of Jesus. Up until that time, the followers of Christ had to depend very largely for their knowledge of the story of Jesus upon "oral tradition," although there were some written records available at a very early date, as Luke indicates in the opening words of his Gospel (Luke 1:1). For the most part, however, in those early days groups of believers would hear the story from the lips of one of the apostles, perhaps. They would pass the message on to others; and these, to still others.

It is reasonable to suppose that Mark sensed the fact that the wonderful stories of Jesus might undergo change and distortion in the constant retelling through the years, if someone did not make a permanent and dependable record of them. And indeed, there would doubtless be occasions when certain groups would have no one in their midst who was intimately acquainted with the basic facts of the life and ministry of Jesus Christ the Lord. If Mark could provide a written record for the use of the churches in that day, it would make the good news of Jesus Christ the Son of God more easily accessible to a larger number of people.

3. *Strength and Comfort for Persecuted Christians*

There was a growing apprehension among the early Christians concerning the martyrdom of the saints. They doubtless were constantly asking, "Why do God's good servants have to die such cruel deaths?" The widely-heralded executions of Paul and Peter were quite fresh in the minds of the Christians of that day. Besides, many of them had been stunned by the ruthless slaughter of their own relatives and friends, for no other reason than that they were Christians. In addition to all of this, Jesus himself, the Son of God, had suffered death upon a cross. How could these things be? The early Christians needed a strong word of encouragement and explanation.

In his Gospel, Mark undertook to give the needed word. Jesus died, Mark declared, because of the hatred and antipathy of the religious leaders of his day. Jesus would not compromise the truth nor stand aside from his divinely appointed mission, even though it should mean his death upon a cross. By the same token, Mark inferred, Christians of every generation must stand firm and unafraid in the face of the most brutal persecution. The way of the Christian is the way of the cross—the way of self-renunciation and self-sacrifice (8:31; 9:31; 10:32-34).

Mark also reveals in his Gospel that Jesus died because he chose to die. For that very purpose he came to earth (10:45). Christ died for the sins of the world. Though he knew that his last journey would terminate in his crucifixion, he nonetheless boldly went forth to meet his enemies there. The death of Jesus was not simply a tragedy. It was all in accordance with the divine purpose to overcome the evil one and effect redemption for sin.

In recording all of this, Mark leaves the clear inference that the sufferings of saints also have a place in the plan and the purpose of God, though to a far less degree. In truth, the blood of the martyrs would become the seed of the church. In their suffering and dying, the saints of that day were lighting a lamp that could never be put out.

4. *The Mighty Works of Jesus*

With such a purpose in mind, Mark proceeded to describe Jesus as "the strong Son of God" who answered the challenge of his critics with mighty deeds and, at the same time, met the crying needs of the multitudes with miraculous works of love and compassion. It has properly been pointed out by biblical scholars that Mark's story of Jesus is much more a record of his deeds than of his words.

It is noteworthy that the extended passages of the teachings of Jesus that occur in Matthew (the Sermon on the Mount, for example), and in John (such as John 14–17) do not appear in Mark's Gospel. Mark is more concerned with what Jesus did in his public ministry than with what he said, and especially with what he did in giving himself for the sins of the world upon the cross of Calvary. The Gospel of Mark is predominately the story of divine action in the midst of a sinful world.

III. THE PLAN OF MARK'S GOSPEL

The Gospel of Mark may be divided into five main sections, which we will further divide as we proceed with our study.

1. *An Introduction* (1:1–20)

Mark begins his book by linking his story with the Old Testament. The Old Testament saints through the centuries had looked for a coming Deliverer whose advent was to be announced by a heaven-sent messenger. By identifying John the Baptist as the promised messenger, Mark indicates that

Jesus was the fulfilment of these prophecies. In his introduction Mark omits any reference to the birth and childhood of Jesus and introduces him in his baptism, showing that at the very outset of his public ministry, God the Father acknowledged Jesus to be his Son.

Mark follows a brief mention of the baptism with an equally brief reference to our Lord's temptation. He does not go into the meaning of this experience. He mentions it and then records the calling of the first disciples.

2. *The Great Galilean Ministry* (1:21 to 6:13)

After his brief introduction, Mark launches out upon a description of our Lord's great Galilean ministry, which possibly extended over a period of about a year and a half. This section of Mark's Gospel begins, after the story of the calling of the first disciples, with an account of several miracles of healing wrought by Jesus (1:21 to 2:12) and continues with a description of the almost immediate opposition to him by the religious leaders (2:15 to 3:6).

After telling of the calling of the twelve (3:13-19), Mark discusses the response of certain groups to the ministry of Jesus (3:20-35); records a few of the parables of Jesus that had to do, chiefly, with the nature of the kingdom of God; describes further miracles; and relates the mission of the twelve.

3. *Ministry in Areas Outside of Galilee* (6:14 to 10:52)

With the death of John the Baptist at the instigation of Herod Antipas (6:14-29), the dark storms of opposition gathered rapidly. Jesus decided to withdraw from his native province of Galilee to avoid facing a crisis at that stage of his public ministry. Besides, he desired to get away from the crowds in order to devote more time to the special training of the twelve. It was during this period that Peter made his "great confession," after which Jesus was transfigured. This section concludes with an account of the last journey to Jerusalem, through Galilee (9:30–50), and Perea and Judea (10:1–52).

4. *Final Ministry in Jerusalem* (11:1 to 14:42)

The dramatic entrance into Jerusalem (11:1–10) brought Jesus into immediate conflict with the religious leaders. He left the city after a long day of controversy, to spend his final hours before the crucifixion with his friends and his disciples.

5. *The Crucifixion and Resurrection* (14:43 to 16:20)

The final section of Mark's Gospel deals with the arrest, trial, crucifixion, and resurrection of Jesus. The entire story moves steadily towards these crowning events—recorded as the supreme evidence of Jesus' devotion to the purpose for which he was sent of the Father to dwell among men.

IV. THE CHARACTERISTICS OF MARK'S GOSPEL

Questions are bound to arise as to how Mark's Gospel differs from the other three Gospels. Does the book of Mark have certain distinguishing characteristics? It certainly does. Some of these may be listed as follows:

1. *The Simple Story of Jesus*

Mark's Gospel is by no means a theological discourse. It is the simple story of the activities of Jesus throughout his public ministry. In keeping with his purpose, Mark's style is direct and forthright and pictorial. He invariably adds a touch of detail here and there that never fails to brighten up his story.

Mark seems to steer clear of giving an interpretation of the outstanding events in the life of our Lord. In the case of the temptation of Jesus, for example, he does not dwell at length upon the significance of this experience in the ministry of Jesus, although it was of tremendous significance. Mark merely records the facts and leaves his readers to make their own interpretation. In the most dramatic and forthright way he tells what happened, but he refrains from going on to tell what these happenings mean for the followers of Jesus Christ throughout the ages. It is partly for this reason that Mark's Gospel is the shortest of the four.

2. *Written for Gentile Believers*

Mark wrote, immediately, for the Christians at Rome and the surrounding areas. To be sure, many of them were converted Jews, but many of them were Gentiles. For that reason, there are several instances in this Gospel where matters of particular concern to the Jews are omitted and matters that would be of special interest to Gentile believers are included. Also for this reason, Mark quotes the Old Testament sparingly and, quite unlike Matthew, he makes scant mention of the fulfilment of prophecy. He speaks in the language of the common man. His style is much less literary than that of the other three Gospel writers. The Gospel of Mark has often been called "the people's Gospel."

3. *The Deity of Jesus*

The mystery of the incarnation is, of course, that Jesus was both human and divine. In Jesus, God tabernacled in human flesh. Mark places great emphasis on the deity of Jesus. At the beginning of his ministry, Mark records, God acknowledged Jesus to be his Son. God repeated this acknowledgment on the Mount of Transfiguration, at the height of Jesus' public ministry. Mark points out, over and over again, that the multitudes who listened to Jesus were profoundly impressed with his uniqueness as a teacher and as a worker of miracles. In every situation, Mark portrays

Jesus as the "strong Son of God," with power over the elements, over demons, over all manner of evil, over his enemies and, finally, with power over death.

4. *The Humanity of Jesus*

Mark also recognized the humanity of Jesus. Mark has a great deal to say about the human emotions of Jesus. He sighed deeply in his spirit (8:12); he looked with anger on his merciless critics (3:5); he was, at times, greatly distressed (14:33); he was much displeased when the disciples sought to turn the little children away from him (10:14); he took those same children up in his arms with all of the tenderness of a parent (10:16); he became weary and needed rest (6:31). According to Mark, the incarnation was very real. Jesus was, of a truth, both God and man.

SUGGESTIONS FOR STUDY AND DISCUSSION

1. The members of the group should be encouraged to formulate in a sentence or two the central purposes of their study of this book. Invite each member to express in his own words exactly what he expects to achieve in this undertaking. Write some of the best of these statements on a chalkboard and invite the class members to discuss them, coming at last to a comprehensive statement which everyone will set down in writing.

2. Urge the class members to begin by reading the entire Gospel in one sitting. Such a procedure will be much more profitable than simply to read the book piecemeal from day to day.

3. Suggest that each of the members bring to the class each night a notebook and pencil, and as the study proceeds compile a personal commentary on the book of Mark for future reference.

4. Encourage each member of the class to read the article on the Gospel of Mark in a good Bible dictionary such as *Harper's Bible Dictionary* or *The Westminster Dictionary of the Bible*. Also urge each member to secure a copy of *A Harmony of the Gospels* by A. T. Robertson or a later book *Gospel Parallels*

edited by Burton H. Throckmorton, Jr., to be used in conjunction with the study of this book.

5. Many Bible students have found it helpful to summarize each chapter of the book of the Bible they are studying in a phrase or two, committing these phrases to memory, so that they are able at any time to turn in their Bibles to the chapter dealing with a subject to which they may desire to refer.

6. It will be found helpful in this study for each person to make his own outline of the Gospel.

7. Care should be taken throughout this study to keep the text of the Gospel constantly in mind. It is all too easy to discuss interesting related topics that arise and thus to miss the opportunity that is afforded to become consciously familiar with the actual message of the Gospel under review at this time.

---

[1] Frederick C. Grant, *The Interpreter's Bible* (Nashville: Abingdon Press, 1951), VII, 620.

CHAPTER 2

I. What "the Gospel" Is (1:1)

II. The Fulfilment of Prophecy (1:2–3)

III. The Role of John the Baptist (1:4–8)
1. John's Message
2. The Response of the People
3. John's Role as a Prophet
4. John's Mission as the Forerunner (vv. 7–8)

IV. The Baptism of Jesus (1:9–11)
1. Approval of John's Ministry
2. Approval of Baptism as a Christian Ordinance
3. A Dedication to His Messianic Ministry
4. The Approval of the Father

V. The Temptation of Jesus (1:12–13)
1. Led of the Spirit
2. Could Jesus Be Tempted?
3. The Significance of the Temptation

VI. Beginning in Galilee (1:14–20)

2

THE BEGINNING OF THE GOSPEL

Mark 1:1–20

WITHOUT ANY elaborate introduction, Mark launches right into the story of the earthly ministry of Jesus. He begins, almost abruptly, with the words, "The beginning of the gospel of Jesus Christ, the Son of God."

I. WHAT "THE GOSPEL" IS (1:1)

The very fact that Mark does not stop to define the meaning of the term gospel indicates that he knew quite well that his readers needed no definition. They had heard the gospel and, hearing it, had opened their hearts to its message and its power, and so had entered into a new fellowship with God and with one another. To the people of Mark's day, the gospel was simply the good news of salvation through Jesus Christ the Lord.

This, of course, is the sense in which the term is used throughout the pages of the New Testament. In Acts 15:7, when Paul and Barnabas visited Jerusalem to make a report on their first missionary journey, the brethren were not a little skeptical of the reported conversion of so many Gentiles to the Christian faith. Peter, with his characteristic boldness, stood by Paul and Barnabas to declare, "Men and brethren, ye know how that a good while ago God made choice among us, that the Gentiles by my mouth should hear the word of the gospel, and believe."

It was in this same sense, as the message of salvation, that

Paul used the term when, in writing to the Corinthians he said, "Moreover, brethren, I declare unto you the gospel . . . by which also ye are saved" (1 Cor. 15:1-2). Someone has well said that Jesus came to preach the gospel, but he also gave us a gospel to preach, by his advent among men, by his death upon the cross for our sins, and by his rising from the grave for our justification. It was Mark's purpose in writing his book to set forth the essential message of salvation as it centered in the story of Jesus Christ the Son of God.

II. THE FULFILMENT OF PROPHECY (1:2-3)

(Cf. Luke 3:1-2)

From the point of view of Mark, the story of Jesus began with the ministry of John the Baptist. But even as Mark begins to tell briefly John's part in setting the stage for the earthly ministry of Jesus, the Gospel writer cannot refrain from making mention of the fact that the message of salvation in Christ Jesus was conceived in the heart of God long, long before the voice of the forerunner was heard crying in the wilderness. This Mark does by referring to two Old Testament passages concerning the coming Lord.

In Malachi 3:1 it is written: "Behold, I will send my messenger, and he shall prepare the way before me: and the Lord, whom ye seek, shall suddenly come to his temple." In Isaiah 40:3 we read: "The voice of him that crieth in the wilderness, Prepare ye the way of the Lord, make straight in the desert a highway for our God."

Thus, in a few brief words, Mark identifies Jesus as the promised Deliverer and John the Baptist as the promised forerunner. In effect, Mark is assenting to the truth that was later to be more clearly expressed by the writer of the Epistle to the Hebrews when he said: "God, who at sundry times and in divers manners spake in time past unto the fathers by the prophets, hath in these last days spoken unto us by his Son" (Heb. 1:1-2).

From the historical point of view, it may be said that the message of salvation began with the saving ministry and message of Jesus Christ. Yet, in the purpose of God, it began the very moment that sin entered into the world to separate man from God—and, indeed, prior to that for, as John puts it in the Revelation, Jesus Christ is the Lamb of God, "slain from the foundation of the world" (Rev. 13:8). The scarlet thread of God's redemptive purpose runs throughout the entire Old Testament. Jesus came in human form to fulfil God's promises to men.

III. THE ROLE OF JOHN THE BAPTIST (1:4–8)
(Cf. Matt. 3:1–6, 11–12; Luke 3:3–6, 15–18)

For centuries the voice of the prophets had been silenced. Then, suddenly, the silence was broken.

1. *John's Message*

Some years ago a series of books was published with the title *If I Had Only One Sermon to Preach*. John the Baptist had only one sermon to preach. It was a bold indictment of the religious faith of his day. It was a call to repentance and confession of sin. It was a challenge to his hearers to bear witness to their repentance by submitting to baptism and thus acknowledging the judgment of God upon their sins.

The Jews of John's day were familiar with baptism. They required Gentiles who embraced the Jewish faith to symbolize their cleansing from their old way of life in the act of baptism. The amazing thing about John's message was that he was asking the Jews to do precisely what they required the Gentiles to do. He was demanding that they turn from their sin to God.

The implications of John's message of repentance followed by baptism were both new and radical. Racially the Jews considered themselves to be God's chosen people but spiritually they had become far removed from God. In the light of the imminence of the kingdom of God, John declared to the Jews that they must enter into a new relationship with God, which new relationship they would symbolize by the act of baptism.

John the Baptist prepared the way, not only for the acceptance by the Jewish people of Jesus as the promised Deliverer, but no less for the message that Jesus himself would preach to all who heard him—the message of a heartfelt religion, the message of repentance and faith. John's message, a message of judgment, paved the way for Jesus' message, a message of redemptive love.

2. *The Response of the People*

It is hard to account for the tremendous response of the people to John's message. Certainly no one must have felt like going to the preacher after he had spoken to say, "I greatly enjoyed your sermon." There was nothing enjoyable about it. It was a strong condemnation of their sins and a clear declaration that the day of judgment was at hand.

Perhaps part of the reason for the ready acceptance of John's ministry was his striking appearance. He had the appearance of a typical Old Testament prophet. Perhaps, also, the crowd responded because of his obvious sincerity. He must have preached in dreadful earnestness. He spoke like a prophet of God.

Beyond all these reasons, however, was the fact that the people of that day were heart-hungry for a message from God. For three hundred years no one had appeared to shake men from their spiritual lethargy. No one had fearlessly declared, "Thus saith the Lord." If, today, a church house here and there is comparatively empty, if people no longer go to its services gladly and expectantly, may it not be because, in part at least, the servant of the Lord does not speak with authority as a messenger of God?

When the great evangelist and preacher, George Whitefield, was getting the people of Edinburgh out of their beds at five o'clock each morning to hear his messages, a man on his way to the tabernacle met David Hume, the Scottish philosopher and skeptic. Surprised at seeing the skeptic going to an evangelistic service, especially at such an early hour, the man said, "I thought you did not believe in the gospel!"

Hume tersely replied as he hurried on, "I don't; but he does."

The preacher who believes his message intensely, with genuine conviction, has the power to persuade others to believe.

3. *John's Role as a Prophet*

John believed himself to be the prophet of the Lord. He lived like a prophet in the vast solitude of the wilderness around the Dead Sea, where he had ample opportunity to be alone with God. Much like Amos who brooded in his mountain seclusion and then at last came thundering down upon the people of Jerusalem to call them from their sinfulness, so John the Baptist brooded over the spiritual plight of his people and looked forward to the day when he could declare that the time of God's judgment and God's deliverance had come.

John dressed like a prophet, wearing a simple cloak of camel's hair tied around him with a leather belt. His very appearance led the people to conclude that this was surely Elijah who had returned from the grave.

In his devotion to his calling, John denied himself of the comforts of life, such as they were in that day, subsisting on the locusts and wild honey that were easily accessible to his hand. While rigorous asceticism is by no means a necessary part of the Christian life, most of us will agree that it is possible to pamper the physical appetite at the expense of the soul.

It is quite possible to underestimate the impact that John the Baptist had upon the people of his day. It is noteworthy that, except for Jesus, Paul, and Peter, the name of John the Baptist is mentioned more often in the New Testament than any other. His appearance was so commanding, his personality so forceful, his message so challenging, and his influence so potent, that even the ruthless and powerful Herod Antipas was afraid of him.

4. *John's Mission as the Forerunner* (vv. 7–8)

John's message was intended not simply to stir the people to repentance but also to make them ready to acknowledge Jesus as the Coming One.

Apparently John was not a little disturbed by the tremendous impression he had made upon the people and by the reception he had received at their hands. It would seem that they were already saying one to the other, "Surely this must be the promised Deliverer." In answer to this point of view, John sought to make it clear that the expected Deliverer, the promised Messiah, was a far greater personality than was he. To compare John the Baptist to the Messiah was, he declared, like comparing a poor and insignificant slave to his affluent master.

Indeed, said John in effect, "I do not merit so much as the rating of a slave for the coming Messiah for, unlike the slave in his service to his master, I am not worthy to untie the shoes of the Coming One."

John the Baptist recognized Jesus to be greater than he, not only in person but in purpose and in mission. John had come to offer a ceremonial baptism that was the outward symbol of an inner experience. Jesus would come to endow those who believe in his name with that inner experience. He would enter into the hearts of believers to make them new creatures. He would, indeed, baptize them with the Holy Spirit.

It was John's desire to give to Jesus a place of eminence that the forerunner would never claim for himself. A few months later John the Baptist pursued this purpose further by saying to some of his disciples who had brought him news concerning the ministry of Jesus in Judea: "Ye yourselves bear me witness, that I said, I am not the Christ, but that I am sent before him. He that hath the bride is the bridegroom: but the friend of the bridegroom, which standeth and heareth him, rejoiceth greatly because of the bridegroom's voice: this my joy therefore is fulfilled. He must increase, but I must decrease" (John 3:28-30).

Perhaps no man was ever more tempted to stand in the bright light of public acclaim than was John. It is a tribute to his strength of character and to his faithfulness to his divinely appointed task, that he was so completely willing to accept the lesser role that had been ordained for him in the purpose of God.

IV. THE BAPTISM OF JESUS (1:9-11)
(Cf. Matt. 3:13-17; Luke 3:21-23)

Having described briefly the mission and the ministry of John the Baptist, Mark now begins to tell the story of Jesus. The public ministry of Jesus began that day when he appeared near the Jordan and submitted himself to John for baptism, saying, in answer to John's vigorous protest, "Suffer it to be so now: for thus it becometh us to fulfil all righteousness" (Matt. 3:15).

The question naturally arises, "Why was Jesus baptized?" What was its significance to him? Obviously, it did not have the same meaning for him as it does for us, since he had no sins to confess and, therefore, no necessity for bearing witness to the experience of a new way of life, as do we. And yet, Jesus' baptism was full of meaning—for Jesus himself, for John, and for all who have believed and been baptized since that day.

1. *Approval of John's Ministry*

To the crowds that went out to hear him, John had preached repentance followed by baptism. In fact, baptism was such a significant part of his message and of his ministry that he became known, not as John the preacher nor even as John the prophet, but as John the Baptist, or John the baptizer. There may very well have been those hearing him, who said within themselves, "The need for repentance we can clearly understand, but why should we submit to baptism?" By coming to John in the presence of all the people, Jesus was saying, in effect, "I agree with your message, and I agree with your insistence upon baptism, to which I gladly submit myself at your hands." Thus did Jesus place his seal of approval upon the work of his forerunner.

2. *Approval of Baptism as a Christian Ordinance*

In submitting to baptism, Jesus also endorsed it as a Christian ordinance. In the new order that he was about to establish, baptism would have a significant place. At the close of his earthly ministry, which he thus began, he would say to his followers in every generation, "Go ye therefore, and teach all nations, baptizing them in the name of the Father, and of the Son, and of the Holy Ghost" (Matt. 28:19). His words would be all the more meaningful and compelling since he himself had passed through the waters of baptism.

3. *A Dedication to His Messianic Ministry*

For thirty years Jesus had lived in comparative privacy. Only once in the New Testament is the curtain drawn aside for us to learn something of his childhood and youth, and then he is not presented as a preacher or a worker of miracles, but as an earnest young inquirer. For the remainder of those thirty years he lived far from the public eye, in the little town of Nazareth and was apparently known to his neighbors only as Jesus, the son of Mary, the carpenter's wife.

From the particular moment of his baptism, Jesus would forever leave behind all of this privacy and obscurity. From that day forward he would be ceaselessly engaged in his mission of teaching and healing and turning the hearts of men from darkness unto light. His name would soon be known throughout the land of his birth and, in due time, throughout the whole world. Surely it is not at all improper to believe that, at the hour of his baptism, he solemnly dedicated himself to the purpose for which he had been sent by the Father to dwell amongst men—the salvation of the world.

Is there not a sense in which the baptism of every devout believer is a moment of dedication? There must be many an individual who will never forget that hour, that hallowed hour, when in obedience to the command of his Lord he made witness not only to Christ's death, burial, and resurrection but also to his own death unto sin and his new life in Christ. Baptism is a moment when each believer must surely say,

> "Take my life and let it be
> Consecrated, Lord, to thee."

4. *The Approval of the Father*

It is quite clear that God took pleasure in the baptism of his Son. Mark records the coming of a voice from heaven saying, "Thou art my beloved Son, in whom I am well pleased" (v. 11). It is significant that the voice spoke in the language of the Scriptures. The words, "Thou art my Son," come from Psalms and are a part of the coronation formula of the messianic King (Psalm 2:7). The phrase "in whom I am well pleased" is part of the description of the Servant of the Lord (Isa. 42:1).

One writer has well said regarding the words from heaven:

> This synthesis is no accident. Here is one who knows himself to be at once the Messiah and the lowly Servant of the Lord. And if Jesus knew, even at his baptism, that as Messiah he must go the way marked out for the Servant of the Lord (Isaiah 53 shows the ending of the road), may we not say that, even then, there must have fallen across his path the shadow of a cross?[1]

V. The Temptation of Jesus (1:12–13)

(Cf. Matt. 4:1–11; Luke 4:1–13)

The light of heaven shone brightly upon the countenance of Jesus as he stepped out of the waters of the Jordan. The approving voice of the Father was ringing in his ears. But soon the light would give place to the shadows of temptation, and the voice that our Lord would hear would be the subtle voice of the tempter for, as Mark records it: "Immediately the spirit driveth him into the wilderness. And he was there in the wilderness forty days, tempted of Satan; and was with the wild beasts; and the angels ministered unto him" (vv. 12–13).

1. *Led of the Spirit*

It is difficult to understand why God would deliberately lead his Son in whom he was well pleased into the wilderness to be tempted. But this he did. It should be remembered that just as soon as Jesus would begin to exert his power against sin and darkness and all manner of evil, the ruler of the powers of darkness would vigorously oppose him. Apparently it was in the divine scheme of things for Jesus to "have it out with Satan" at the very beginning, to convince Satan that nothing would thwart the Saviour in his purpose.

It has often been said that surely God will not lead us into temptation. No, but we are mere humans. We might all too easily lose the battle. After all, we are no match for Satan;

but Jesus was. He would come out unscathed, and Satan would discover surely that Christ was and is a light shining in the darkness that the darkness simply cannot put out.

2. *Could Jesus Be Tempted?*

How could Jesus Christ the Son of God be subjected to temptation? Was it at all possible for him to sin?

John A. Broadus, in his timeless *Commentary on the Gospel of Matthew,* gives this answer to such an inquiry:

> If we think of his human nature in itself, apart from the co-linked divinity, and apart from the Holy Spirit that filled and led him, then we must say that, like Adam in his state of purity, like the angels and every other moral creature, his humanity was certainly in itself capable of sinning, and thus the temptation was real, and was felt as such, and as such was overcome; while yet in virtue of the union with the divine nature, and of the power of the Holy Spirit that filled him, it was morally impossible that he should sin.[2]

In a sense, therefore, the temptation was a proof of Jesus' real humanity; and his unqualified victory over the adversary was, no less, a proof of his real deity.

3. *The Significance of the Temptation*

The temptation of Jesus by Satan in the wilderness was vitally related to his messianic ministry. Jesus came into the world to die for the world and by his death (and resurrection) to provide eternal life for all who would believe in his name. It was at this very point that Satan assailed our Lord.

In effect, by the three temptations that he brought before Jesus, Satan was saying: "Give up your way of saving the world. It is the way of suffering and sacrifice and death. Try my way; it is the way of self-service, and self-protection, and self-aggrandizement."

It may be said that, in his refusal to yield to Satan's offers,

Jesus, then and there, won the victory of the cross. Luke records that Satan left Jesus "for a season" (Luke 4:13). But it was only for a season. Throughout his Gospel, Mark presents Jesus as being continually in conflict with Satan and his representatives and with the powers of evil.

VI. Beginning in Galilee (1:14–20)
(Cf. Matt. 4:12, 17–22; Luke 4:14–15; 5:1–11)

Jesus was now ready to embark upon his public work. Mark omits the early Judean ministry that occupied a brief period following the baptism (see John 2:13 to 4:3). He does indicate that Jesus left Judea when he heard that John the Baptist had been imprisoned (1:14). It is believed by some that the opposition to John was a foregleam of opposition to the one whom John had publicly introduced. Not willing at the moment to clash openly with the religious leaders in Jerusalem, Jesus quietly withdrew to the regions around Galilee. The time had not yet come for the issue to be clearly drawn between him and the rulers of the Jews. When that time did come, he would meet it with courage and with power.

Jesus introduced his ministry of preaching with the words, "The time is fulfilled, and the kingdom of God is at hand: repent ye, and believe the gospel" (v. 15). He was thus announcing that by the preaching of the gospel and by Christ's ministry among men, God would exercise his reign in the hearts of men. Men would open their hearts to the reign of God by repentance and faith.

At the very beginning of his public ministry, Jesus gathered around him an inner group of followers upon whom he would direct his special concern and to whom he would commit, in a special way, the task that he would do through human channels following his death and resurrection. The first disciples were simple men, engaged in the simple task of catching fish in the clear blue waters of the Sea of Galilee.

Jesus called men who were busy with their own work that they might become busy with his work.

Simon was a born leader. Someone has said of Simon Peter that he was always striking twelve o'clock—sometimes the twelve of midnight, as when he shamefully denied his Lord, and sometimes the twelve of noonday, as when he boldly confessed that Jesus was indeed "the Christ, the Son of the living God."

Andrew, Simon's brother, was an entirely different sort of man. His great gift was that of bringing others to Jesus— first his own brother, then the lad with the loaves and fishes, then the inquiring Greeks. He was a master of the art of winning others to his Lord.

John was a man of spiritual insight. Though he was a man of passion, a "son of thunder," he was to become known as the beloved disciple.

James was a man of real courage and devotion. He was to be the first of the twelve apostles to become a martyr to the cause of Christ.

These first four disciples were different in temperament, in gifts, and in fitness for the various roles that they would be called upon to fulfil. It is even so in this our day. God takes us as we are, with the gifts that we have, and transforms us by his grace and asks each of us to use his individual abilities in the service of the kingdom. God asks only that we respond to his call to our hearts with the same forthrightness as these first four responded to Christ's call to them when "straightway they forsook their nets, and followed him."

May we not push the comparison further? As Jesus called these disciples he promised, "Come ye after me and I will make you to become fishers of men" (v. 17). For Peter the divine plan involved public preaching, as at Pentecost when thousands were converted. For Andrew it involved the personal ministries already mentioned. For James, the call was ultimately to include administrative leadership in Jerusalem. For John, we believe it involved a long pastorate at Ephesus. But, varied as their services were, all four disciples were promised equally the designation "fishers of men." Should not you and I be candidates for the same "degree" in whatever capacity we are called upon to serve?

SUGGESTIONS FOR STUDY AND DISCUSSION

1. Discuss the meaning of the term "the gospel of Jesus Christ." What do people usually mean when they say of a minister, "He does not preach the gospel?"

2. Examine some of the more significant messianic prophecies in the Old Testament. In what sense was Jesus actually the "Messiah of Israel"? In what respects was he unlike the deliverer they had expected?

3. With the help of a concordance, look up each reference in the Gospels to John the Baptist, and then write in your notebook a brief account of his life and work.

4. Discuss the significance of the baptism of Jesus.

5. Read all three accounts of the temptation of Jesus. In your own words formulate what you believe to be the real significance of the temptation in the life and work of Jesus.

6. It is suggested that you begin your own outline of the Third Gospel, as proposed on page 15. Consider Mark 1:1–20. What seem to you the significant divisions? Will you write your own outline in your notebook and commit it to memory?

7. As has been suggested, making an outline is an activity which is to many people an intriguing plan for Bible study. If you prefer some other activity, you may like to do one of the following:
    (1) Select and underline what you consider to be the key verses in each chapter or section.
    (2) Make a list of key words to help you recall the contents of each chapter.

8. Draw or trace an outline map of Palestine in the days of Jesus' earthly ministry. As each chapter in Mark is read, add to your

map the places mentioned, so that your map becomes a cumulative record of your study of the whole book.

---

[1] Archibald M. Hunter, *The Gospel According to Saint Mark* (New York: The Macmillan Company, 1953), p. 29.

[2] Alvah Hovey, *An American Commentary on the New Testament* (Philadelphia: The American Baptist Publication Society [The Judson Press], 1886), I, 61. Used by permission.

CHAPTER 3

I. Jesus' Healing Ministry Begins (1:21–45)

1. The Man with the Unclean Spirit (vv. 21–28)
2. Peter's Mother-in-law (vv. 29–34)
3. The Cure of a Leper (vv. 35–45)

II. Growing Opposition to Jesus (2:1 to 3:6)

1. Criticized for Forgiving Sin (2:1–12)
2. Criticized for Dealing with Publicans (2:13–17)
3. Criticized for Refusing to Fast (2:18–22)
4. Criticized for Breaking the Sabbath (2:23 to 3:6)

III. The Response to Jesus' Ministry (3:7–35)

1. Response of the Multitudes (vv. 7–12)
2. Response of His Disciples (vv. 13–19)
3. Response of His Family (vv. 20–21; 31–35)
4. Response of the Religious Leaders (vv. 22–30)

IV. Teaching in Parables (4:1–34)

1. Parable of the Sower (vv. 1–20)
2. Parable of the Lamp (vv. 21–25)
3. Parable of the Seed Growing Secretly (vv. 26–29)
4. Parable of the Mustard Seed (vv. 30–34)

V. Further Miracles of Jesus (4:35 to 5:43)

1. Stilling the Storm (4:35–41)
2. The Gadarene Demoniac (5:1–20)
3. Jairus' Daughter (5:21–23; 35–43)
4. A Woman in Dire Need (5:24–34)

VI. Closing Ministry in Galilee (6:1–13)

1. In the Synagogue at Nazareth (vv. 1–6)
2. The Mission of the Twelve (vv. 7–13)

3

THE GREAT GALILEAN MINISTRY

Mark 1:21 to 6:13

MARK's record of the public ministry of Jesus begins in the province of Galilee. This province was in the northern section of Palestine, to the west of the Jordan. It was a comparatively small area, some fifty miles long and thirty miles wide. The Jewish historian, Josephus, tells us that it possessed some two hundred and four cities and villages, the smallest of which numbered 15,000 inhabitants. It was an exceedingly fertile area and its life centered about the beautiful Sea of Galilee whose waters furnished a bountiful supply of fish. There were nine fair-sized towns clustered around the Sea of Galilee, one of which was Capernaum.[1]

Jesus apparently chose Galilee for his extended public ministry of teaching and healing, for two main reasons:

In the first place, while the Galileans in general were devoutly religious, they were not nearly so much under the domination of the religious and the political leaders of the day as were the people of Jerusalem and Judea. The highways of commerce ran through Galilee, with the result that the Galileans came in contact with a constant stream of travelers from Egypt, Arabia, Syria and other places. With their larger experience and broader outlook, it was only to be expected that the people of Galilee would gladly hear what Jesus had to say to them—at least, more gladly than would their more conservative countrymen to the south.

In the second place, Galilee was the scene of Jesus' child-

34 A STUDY OF THE GOSPEL OF MARK

hood. In going there, he was going back home. He would give to Galilee the opportunity that Judea was not yet ready nor willing to receive.

I. JESUS' HEALING MINISTRY BEGINS (1:21–45)
(Cf. Matt. 8:14–17; 4:23–25; 8:2–4; Luke 4:38 to 5:16)

It is quite significant that Mark begins his record of the happenings in Galilee by pointing out that, "straightway on the sabbath day he [Jesus] entered into the synagogue, and taught" (v. 21). The people were profoundly impressed on this occasion, not so much it would seem by what Jesus said, as by the way in which he said it. The scribes, to whom they ordinarily listened, found their authority in the traditions of the elders. Jesus spoke as one who, himself, was the authority. They felt keenly that, of a truth, he knew whereof he spoke.

1. *The Man with the Unclean Spirit* (vv. 21–28)

The teaching of Jesus in the synagogue was abruptly interrupted by a man who was possessed of an unclean spirit. From the large place that Mark gives to the miracles of healing in the ministry of Jesus, it might be assumed that Jesus conceived himself, in the beginning of his public work, to be primarily a healer. This is not the case. Primarily he was the Redeemer, as it was declared to Joseph, "Thou shalt call his name Jesus: for he shall save his people from their sins" (Matt. 1:21).

As the Redeemer, Jesus addressed himself first of all to teaching, such teaching as had never before been heard. He had a startling new message for the people—a startling new interpretation of what it meant to be a servant of God.

As Jesus well knew, his time was short until he would face the cross. He had much to teach, and he must take advantage of every opportunity to teach it. At first thought, it seems as though he was continually diverted from his direct teaching ministry by the urgent appeal of human need, yet he apparently used each case of need as a means of teaching. The physical condition of many of the people of Palestine in that day was appalling. Medical practice was crude at best, and what medical practice there was, was often thwarted by traditional religious regulations that were largely concerned with ceremonial cleanness and outward conformity.

As Jesus stood in the midst of human suffering, he could do nothing other than to meet that need with the power that was his as the Son of God. Well did he know that many of the people who came to him came not to hear about the kingdom of God nor to discover how they might enter into it. They came to get rid of their infirmities, and always Jesus was moved with compassion and answered their appeal. So, in the synagogue, Jesus released the tormented man from the domination of an unclean spirit, but not before the unclean spirit had announced to the people of Nazareth that Jesus was the "Holy One of God" (v. 24).

At this time in his ministry, Jesus did not publicly announce in so many words that he was the Messiah, the Son of God. He preferred that his hearers should come to this conviction for themselves in the light of the words that he said and the deeds that he wrought. Apparently, the people in the synagogue did not grasp the significance of this announcement, since they said no further word about it, though some of them may have recalled it later as Jesus' fame spread abroad.

2. *Peter's Mother-in-law* (vv. 29–34)

Later in the day, Jesus healed Peter's mother-in-law, who was sick of a fever. She arose immediately and ministered unto Jesus and her other guests.

The news of the healing of the man with the unclean spirit, in the synagogue, spread quickly throughout the community. By nightfall, as Mark records: "All the city was gathered together at the door. And he healed many that were sick of divers diseases, and cast out many devils" (vv. 33–34).

It did not take the people long to discover the presence of Jesus in their midst nor to realize that he had the power to rid them of their sickness and their infirmities. By the close of the first day of his public ministry in Galilee, his fame had already been noised abroad.

3. *The Cure of a Leper* (vv. 35–45)

The following morning, "rising up a great while before day" (v. 35), Jesus departed into a solitary place to pray. This practice seems to have been his custom. On occasions he would spend all night in prayer. This he did, apparently, because he felt the need of quiet communion with the Father. In so doing, Jesus set an example for his disciples in every generation. The greater the stress and anxiety that life places upon us, the busier we are, the more do we need to make a place in our day for quiet communion with God.

Soon Jesus was interrupted by the disciples, who came to tell him that everybody was looking for him. In response he set out upon a preaching tour of the towns and villages of Galilee. At this stage of his ministry, he made it a practice to visit the synagogues wherever he went. In one of these synagogues, a leper came kneeling to him. With a word Jesus healed the man and sent him on his way rejoicing.

II. GROWING OPPOSITION TO JESUS (2:1 to 3:6)
(Cf. Matt. 9:1–17; 12:1–14; Luke 5:17 to 6:11)

At this point, it would not have been surprising if Mark had gone on to record that the religious leaders were glad that their people were being so greatly helped and encouraged. That was not the case, however. Immediately, the scribes and Pharisees began to sense a threat to their security and a challenge to their religious traditions. So, instead of praising Jesus, they began to criticize him.

1. *Criticized for Forgiving Sin* (2:1-12)

The criticism of the leaders first became vocal when Jesus looked at the man "sick of the palsy," whose four friends had ingeniously contrived to bring him to Jesus by letting him down through the roof. Jesus, seeing that the man's infirmity was rooted in sin, dealt first, not with his physical sickness, but with his spiritual sickness and pronounced him forgiven of his sins. Right away, the scribes set up a protest. "Look here," they said in effect, "only God can forgive sin." How right they were! Their error lay in the fact that they would not recognize Jesus as the Messiah of God. The onlookers had more insight than their religious leaders, for they, at least, gave the glory to God (v. 12).

2. *Criticized for Dealing with Publicans* (2:13-17)

Once begun, the opposition of the scribes and the Pharisees steadily mounted. A little later on—just how soon we do not know—Jesus saw Levi, the son of Alphaeus (commonly known to us as Matthew) engaged in his work as a tax collector, or publican.

How the Jews despised the publicans! In the eyes of the Jews, the publicans had sold their racial birthright for "a mess of pottage" by agreeing to collect the taxes from the Jewish people, on a commission basis, for the Roman government.

Jesus invited Matthew to follow him and, to make matters worse in the opinion of the leaders, Jesus accepted an invitation to a dinner attended largely by "publicans and sinners" —people who did not comply with the religious tradition of the Jewish faith.

3. *Criticized for Refusing to Fast* (2:18-22)

Jesus' association with Matthew and his friends was too much for the Pharisees, but they did not approach Jesus at that moment. They waited until they could challenge him on some other grounds. The occasion soon presented itself.

Some of "the disciples of John and of the Pharisees" noticed that the disciples of Jesus did not observe the Jewish regulations concerning fasting. To the Pharisees, this was unthinkable. Fasting was a significant part of their religious life. They probably reasoned that, if Jesus was in truth a religious prophet or teacher, he could not so lightly permit his disciples to set aside such a central religious tradition.

Jesus' answer was clear and straightforward. He did not come to enforce the outward forms of the older order but to start a new order which would fulfil that which the old had foreshadowed (v. 21). To be sure, Jesus would at times fast, but for him fasting was not simply a religious rite required by law. It was an affair of the heart. It was the natural outcome of his prior devotion to prayer and spiritual communion with the Father.

4. *Criticized for Breaking the Sabbath* (2:23 to 3:6)

It was not long before the Pharisees were again voicing their complaint against Jesus for failing to observe their traditions. This time it was his failure to observe the sabbath. His disciples had plucked some grain while passing through a field on a sabbath day. This was strictly contrary to the Jewish laws against sowing, garnering, or threshing grain on the sabbath.

Jesus answered the criticism of the religious leaders with an illustration from their own Scriptures, the Old Testament. Then he set forth the Christian principle for the observance of the Lord's Day as he said, "The sabbath was made for man, and not man for the sabbath" (2:27). The Lord's Day is not a burden to be borne but a day of rest and worship to be used and enjoyed.

Jesus did not allow the criticism of the Pharisees to thwart him in his spiritual ministry in the least for, when he again entered the synagogue on a sabbath day, and saw there a man with a withered hand, a human being in need, he challenged the Pharisees with a look of anger and went ahead to restore the man's hand "whole as the other" (3:5). The Pharisees then began to make definite plans to destroy Jesus (3:6).

III. THE RESPONSE TO JESUS' MINISTRY (3:7-35)
(Cf. Matt. 12:15-37, 46-50; Luke 6:12-16; 8:19-21)

The response to Jesus' ministry was by no means wholly negative. There were a great many who were attracted by his works and his words. In the ensuing section of his Gospel, Mark goes on to describe the response to the ministry of Jesus in several specific instances.

1. *Response of the Multitudes* (vv. 7-12)

The common people were, for the most part, greatly moved by the ministry of Jesus. They crowded around him wherever he went. Try as he would to get rest and to engage in fellowship with his disciples and in communion with the Father, Jesus simply could not get away from the surging throng. When he withdrew to the sea, they followed him, coming from widely scattered areas (vv. 7-8).

Mark notes that "they pressed upon him for to touch him, as many as had plagues. And unclean spirits, when they saw him, fell down before him, and cried, saying, Thou art the Son of God" (vv. 10-11).

2. *Response of His Disciples* (vv. 13-19)

A chosen few turned to Jesus, not so much for what they could get from him as for what they could give to him. They sought him not simply as their benefactor but as their Lord and Master. So, at last, when Jesus could get away from the crowds, he called about him twelve men and empowered them "that they should be with him, and that he might send them forth to preach, and to have power to heal sicknesses, and to cast out devils" (vv. 14–15).

Throughout his earthly ministry, when so many people refused to commit themselves wholly to Jesus, what a comfort it must have been to him to have at least a little handful who followed him because they loved him and desired sincerely to serve him. Mark later tells us that there were still other faithful followers who mingled with the crowds that surged around Jesus. Among them were many women who gladly ministered to him and his disciples.

3. *Response of His Family* (vv. 20–21; 31–35)

Unfortunately, the members of Jesus' family were not numbered amongst his faithful followers. The word translated "friends" (v. 21) may better be translated "family." The other members of the household of Mary and Joseph did not acknowledge Jesus' messiahship, nor did they sympathize with his ministry. They frankly sought to lay hold of him, apparently to take him back home with them.

Jesus took this occasion to inform his listeners that true kinship with him is determined, not by the ties of blood, but by spiritual union with him. All who have been born into the family of God through faith in Jesus Christ are Jesus' brothers and, no less, brothers one of another.

4. *Response of the Religious Leaders* (vv. 22–30)

The religious leaders continued to oppose Jesus. They came forth to criticize him mercilessly. They accused him of being in league with Beelzebub "the prince of the devils" (v. 22).

Much has been said concerning what Jesus meant by the statement, "But he that shall blaspheme against the Holy

Ghost hath never forgiveness" (v. 29). This has commonly been referred to as "the unpardonable sin," though that precise term does not appear anywhere in the Scriptures. How many people have lived in mortal fear that they have committed the unpardonable sin and have refused to accept Christ because they believe that he will not forgive them!

Granting that the words of Jesus had a special application to the attitude of the scribes and Pharisees at that time (which is really an involved and difficult problem) we may see that the meaning for us would seem to be this: The sin that may not be forgiven is the sin of deliberate, persistent unbelief—the refusal to accept Jesus Christ as the Son of God and the Saviour of men and the failure to recognize the Holy Spirit as the Spirit of God who alone can enter into human hearts to redeem them. There is no pardon for the man who will not enter into the family of God through faith in Jesus Christ.

From the practical point of view, there is in actuality no sin that God will not forgive except the sin of unbelief and rejection. No matter how low a man has sunk nor how grievously he has transgressed the laws of God, he may be forgiven—on one condition. He must believe in the Lord Jesus Christ to be saved.

IV. TEACHING IN PARABLES (4:1–34)

(Cf. Matt. 13:1–53; Luke 8:4–18)

Mark now turns, for a while, from the miracles of Jesus to the teaching of Jesus by parable. One definition of a parable is that it is an earthly story with a heavenly meaning. It is perhaps more accurate to say that a parable is a "brief story told by way of comparison to present some central truth." Jesus took the simple things of life, things with which all of his hearers were quite familiar, and used them to enforce profound and meaningful spiritual truths.

1. Parable of the Sower (vv. 1–20)

Who of Jesus' listeners had not seen a farmer striding through his field, scattering seed right and left? Some of the seed would fall on the pathway, to be eaten by the birds; some, on the hard ground, to be scorched by the rays of the sun; some, upon a shallow layer of earth that lay on a bed of rock, so that there was no room for rootage; some, among the thorns and briars, only to be choked out; and some, of course, on good rich soil to bear an abundant fruitage.

So it is always with those who preach the gospel. The spiritual fruitage of the message they preach will quite largely be determined by the sort of response it finds in the hearts of those who hear it. How true this has been in all the centuries since the day in which Jesus first uttered these words!

Jesus' explanation to his disciples of the reason he used parables is, at first, somewhat difficult to understand. John A. Broadus in his *Commentary on Mark* is quite helpful at this point:

> While illustrating the truth to those who were spiritual and eager to know, the parables would make it obscure to those who were unspiritual and unwilling to be taught. Our Lord is speaking a few hours after the blasphemous accusation. The malignant opposition of his enemies had reached the height of outrageous insult and unpardonable blasphemy. To these, the parables will be a deserved judgment—while persons wishing to know can seek explanation.[2]

2. Parable of the Lamp (vv. 21–25)

Those who heard the parable of the sower may very well have asked, in their hearts, "If many will not listen to our testimony concerning the things of God, why then should we go to the trouble of bearing witness at all?"

Jesus answered any such question in a brief parabolic illustration, saying, in effect: "You have no choice. You must bear witness. You must let the light of God's grace and God's presence so shine that men who live in darkness may come to know and to embrace the true light." What a privilege to know, in one's own personal experience, the good news of salvation! And what a responsibility!

3. *Parable of the Seed Growing Secretly* (vv. 26-29)

After all, Jesus went on to imply in his next parable, who is to say that men do not respond to our witness of the gospel? You never know. A word in behalf of Christ spoken today may not bear fruit for years to come and then, suddenly, a sinner is converted and he affirms that the message he received years ago has, at last, borne fruit. The growth of the kingdom is not observable. It is God's unseen work in the hearts of men.

This parable would indicate that it is our business as the servants of Jesus Christ, not to measure the results of our witness, but to sow the good seed. "In due season we shall reap, if we faint not" (Gal. 6:9). The silent testimony of a godly mother or a godly father may one day win a son or a daughter to Christ, after many intervening years.

4. *Parable of the Mustard Seed* (vv. 30-34)

Jesus went on to exhort his hearers not to be discouraged by small results, nor by seemingly slow progress in the growth of God's reign in the hearts of men and women. Perhaps he was thinking of his own earthly ministry. As yet, his name and his work were known only within the confines of the little land of Palestine. It was a comparatively small beginning, but there would come a time when his words would be cherished and his name adored and his quickening touch felt around the world. From the tiniest of seeds, a towering shrub would grow.

We do the cause of Christ a disservice when we belittle the influence of the gospel throughout the centuries. To be sure, evil is still with us on every hand. Much remains to be done. But, thanks be unto God, much has already been done, in Jesus' name. Even in lands where our missionaries worked for years, only to have their work interrupted and the doors of further opportunity closed against them, we may yet see that their work has not been in vain. The seed of the gospel, faithfully sown, will continue to bear fruit.

V. FURTHER MIRACLES OF JESUS (4:35 to 5:43)
   (Cf. Matt. 8:18, 23-34; 9:18-26; Luke 8:22-56)

Once more, Jesus decided to retire from the surging multitudes. He suggested to his disciples that they cross to the other side of the Sea of Galilee.

1. *Stilling the Storm* (4:35-41)

We are inclined to think of the beautiful Sea of Galilee as quiet and placid. Actually, it is subject to violent storms. As the wind comes rushing through the mountain ravines, it sometimes strikes the waters of Galilee with tremendous force. We are told that, until this day, a storm on Galilee is a terrifying experience for many a traveler.

That evening, when the storm came down upon the disciples they were genuinely frightened, but they felt sure that Jesus could handle the situation so they hurriedly awakened him from his sleep. At his words the storm subsided. Then he gently chided them for their lack of faith.

Could this simple incident have been a portent of the things to come? Was Jesus quietly suggesting to his disciples that, in the days ahead, when the storms of opposition, and doubt, and fear would threaten to engulf them, they should in like manner turn to him in faith?

2. *The Gadarene Demoniac* (5:1-20)

Arriving on the other side of the lake, Jesus and his disciples soon came upon a man who was in sore straits. He was demon-possessed. He was so disturbed by his condition and torment that he felt he must be the victim of no less than a legion of evil spirits. It was a stubborn case. At first, it would seem, the demons refused to obey the command of Jesus. But, at last, they yielded and the man was restored.

Questions have been raised about the stampeding of the herd of swine in connection with this incident. It is best, perhaps, to consider this as a part of the possessed man's complete cure. Perhaps his tormented soul needed the added assurance that he had indeed been released from the domination of the demons. The tragic end of the herd of swine would assure him of the certain destruction of the demons that had molested him.

If the destruction of the herd of swine was a source of a comfort to the possessed man, it certainly was quite the opposite to the men who tended the swine. Fearing lest a further calamity might befall them and their possessions at the hands of Jesus, they urgently demanded that he leave the vicinity.

We sympathize with these men at the financial loss that they (or their masters) had sustained. Yet, we cannot refrain from the thought that throughout the centuries since that day, some people have, at times, been too much inclined to put material values above human values. These swineherders seem to have cared not at all that a poor demented individual had been granted a new lease upon life.

3. *Jairus' Daughter* (5:21–23; 35–43)

When Jesus and his disciples returned to Galilee, they were met by a man named Jairus. He was probably the president of the synagogue and, as such, was responsible for the upkeep of the building and the oversight of the services. He was, therefore, a man of prominence in his community (probably Capernaum). But his social prominence was, at that moment, of little comfort to him, for his daughter was at the point of death. He besought Jesus to heal her.

As the little group journeyed to the house of the ruler of the synagogue, they were met with the news that the little girl had died. It was probably to minister comfort to the heart of Jairus that Jesus said, "The damsel is not dead, but sleepeth" (5:39). By these words he was apparently signifying to Jairus that he had not really lost his daughter. He would again hear the ring of her laughter, and again know the warmth of her affection. Her death would be but a brief sleep from which she would soon arise.

Alone at the bedside of the child, Jesus uttered words that were full of tenderness as he said, "Damsel, I say unto thee, arise" (v. 41). And, forthwith, she arose. This is the first instance of a resurrection from the dead in the New Testament and the only one (apart from the resurrection of Jesus) which Mark records.

4. *A Woman in Dire Need* (5:24–34)

On the way to the house of Jairus, Jesus was surrounded by a great crowd. They pressed him on every side. In the midst of the confusion, he was conscious of one touch that had a purpose. A woman who had been sick for twelve years sought healing. Mark points out that she had spent all that she had in an effort to be cured, but all to no avail (v. 26). She now felt that there was one last hope for her. With remarkable faith she declared, "If I may touch but his clothes, I shall be whole" (v. 28). Her faith was fully rewarded as Jesus said, "Daughter, thy faith hath made thee whole; go in peace, and be whole of thy plague" (v. 34).

VI. CLOSING MINISTRY IN GALILEE (6:1–13)

(Cf. Matt. 13:54–58; 9:35 to 11:1; Luke 9:1–6)

Mark records that, after raising Jairus' daughter from the dead, Jesus "came into his own country," that is, into Galilee.

1. *In the Synagogue at Nazareth* (vv. 1-6)

Returning to Nazareth, Jesus, as his custom was, visited the synagogue. Many who heard him there were astonished at his teaching, but some were skeptical. They simply could not believe that the young man who had grown up in their own community, in the home of Joseph the carpenter and his wife Mary, could have the authority and the miraculous power that were attributed to him.

There has been much discussion as to whether Mary had children other than Jesus, who was conceived of the Holy Spirit. Some insist that she did not. It is true that the words translated "brother" and "sisters" were used to include also half brothers and half sisters. So it is argued that James, Joses, Juda, and Simon, and the sisters, were not Mary's children, but, rather, the children of Joseph by a former marriage. The Scriptures give no proof for this claim.

It is recorded concerning the ministry of Jesus at Nazareth on this particular occasion that "he could there do no mighty work. . . . And he marvelled because of their unbelief" (vv. 5-6).

2. *The Mission of the Twelve* (vv. 7-13)

Before he sent them forth, Jesus invested the twelve with power over unclean spirits as well as with power to heal the sick. He commanded them to make their journey on faith, depending for food and lodging on the kindness of the people to whom they ministered.

For some time the disciples had been constantly in the presence of Jesus as he taught and healed and wrought other miracles. This period had been for them a time of training for the task they would eventually be asked to take over. How well had they learned the lessons that their Master had taught them? Mark records that they had indeed learned them quite well: "And they cast out many devils, and anointed with oil many that were sick, and healed them" (v. 13). With this report, Mark brings to a close the public ministry of Jesus in Galilee. Later he does give us a brief word which seems to indicate something of the satisfaction the disciples felt in "making a report" of their activities after the preaching tour in Galilee was over. And the apostles gathered themselves together unto Jesus, and told him all things, both what they had done, and what they had taught" (Mark 6:30).

SUGGESTIONS FOR STUDY AND DISCUSSION

1. In the second half of the first chapter (vv. 23–45), Mark records three miracles of healing, without comment as to their significance. Name the three miracles. As you think of each one, seek to determine what observing Jesus working that miracle must have meant to the disciples who had so recently begun to follow Jesus and had just listened to his teaching in Capernaum. In each miracle, name the area or force over which Jesus demonstrated his power. Why was such demonstration of particular significance to the disciples at this time?

2. Name the things for which the enemies of Jesus criticized him, as recorded in Mark 2:1 to 3:6. In each instance have someone in the class take the role of one of the criticizers: a scribe (2:6), a scribe or a Pharisee (2:16), a disciple of John the Baptist (2:18), a Pharisee (2:24), or someone in the congregation (3:2). Each person, in his role, should try to tell his point of view as he saw and heard Jesus in the situation described.

3. In his third chapter Mark describes the response that three different groups made to Jesus' ministry. Name these groups and indicate the nature of the response in each case. It will be stimulating to do this by role playing.

4. Give the meaning, as you see it, of each of the four parables recorded in Mark 4:1–34.

5. Indicate what, to you, is the most significant thing in each of the four miracles described in Mark 4:35 to 4:43.

6. In your notebook make your own outline of Mark 1:21 to 6:13, using the outline of this chapter as it proves helpful.

---

[1] Ernest Trice Thompson, *The Gospel According to Mark* (Richmond: John Knox Press, 1954), p. 45.

[2] John A. Broadus, *Commentary on the Gospel of Mark* (Philadelphia: The American Baptist Publication Society, [The Judson Press] 1905), p. 32.

CHAPTER 4

I. THE DEATH OF JOHN (6:14–29)

II. THE FIRST WITHDRAWAL (6:30 to 7:23)
   1. Feeding the Five Thousand (6:35–44)
   2. Jesus Walking on the Sea (6:45–52)
   3. Return to Galilee (6:53–56)
   4. Ceremonial Defilement (7:1–23)

III. THE SECOND WITHDRAWAL (7:24–30)

IV. WITHDRAWAL FROM PHOENICIA (7:31 to 8:12)
   1. Cure of the Deaf Mute (7:31–37)
   2. Feeding the Four Thousand (8:1–9)
   3. Brief Visit to Galilee (8:10–12)

V. THE FOURTH WITHDRAWAL (8:13 to 9:29)
   1. Warning Against the Doctrine of the Pharisees (8:13–21)
   2. The Blind Man at Bethsaida (8:22–26)
   3. The Great Confession (8:27–33)
   4. The Way of Discipleship (8:34 to 9:1)
   5. The Transfiguration (9:2–8)
   6. A Question About Elijah (9:9–13)
   7. The Powerless Disciples (9:14–29)

4

WITHDRAWING FROM GALILEE

Mark 6:14 to 9:29

AFTER the preaching tour by the twelve, Jesus began to withdraw from Galilee as the scene of his public ministry. There were probably several reasons for this new departure. Many of the people of Galilee were intent upon forcing him to be their king and deliverer. Jesus desired to avoid any such public demonstration. He desired to get away from the milling crowds in order to devote more time to the training of the twelve. The time was short; the disciples still had much to learn.

Perhaps the deciding factor in the decision of Jesus no longer to make his headquarters at Capernaum in Galilee was the news of John the Baptist's tragic death and the resulting interest and curiosity that Herod Antipas, tetrarch of Galilee, was showing in Jesus.

I. THE DEATH OF JOHN (6:14–29)
   (Cf. Matt. 14:1–12; Luke 9:7–9)

The story of the execution of John the Baptist is, apart from the record of Jesus' trial and crucifixion, one of the darkest pages in the New Testament. Herod Antipas had at one time visited his half brother, Herod Philip, in Rome. There he persuaded Philip's wife, Herodias, to desert her husband, while Herod Antipas deserted his wife to marry Herodias. It was a scandalous arrangement, contrary both to the laws of the Jews and the laws of God.

John the Baptist boldly denounced the whole affair, with the result that he was thrown into prison at the fortress of Machaerus. In spite of his debased character, Herod Antipas maintained a certain awesome respect for the fearless preacher and was, apparently, not at all inclined to do any more than to keep John in prison.

Herodias had nothing but hatred for John, so she waited for "a convenient day" (v. 21) when she might persuade her husband to put an end to John's life. That occasion presented itself when Herod invited the nobles of his realm to his castle at Machaerus to celebrate his birthday. After his stepdaughter had danced for his guests, Herod, probably in a drunken stupor, offered to give the girl anything she might ask of him up to one half of his kingdom. Actually, he was powerless to dispose of any of his royal estate without the express permission of the Emperor in Rome, under whom Herod held office as a tributary sovereign or "tetrach."

Herodias took this opportunity to get even with John, and, at her suggestion, Salome (whose name we learn from the Jewish historian Josephus) requested the head of John the Baptist on a platter. The moment that Salome expressed her wish, Herod regretted the rash promise he had made. To save face with his guests, however, and because he believed that an oath was binding no matter how ill-advised it might be, he ordered that John should, then and there, be beheaded.

When word came of the wonders that Jesus was performing, not far from Machaerus, the face of John the Baptist rose accusingly before Herod. Surely, he thought, John had risen from the grave to torment him, and perhaps, indeed, to punish him for his evil deed. The inference is that Jesus decided, in the light of Herod's guilty fears, that it was wise to leave the territory of Herod's dominion for "his time had not yet come."

II. THE FIRST WITHDRAWAL (6:30 to 7:23)

(Cf. Matt. 14:13 to 15:20; Luke 9:10–17; John 6:1–21; 7:1)

After the twelve made the report of their tour (v. 30), Jesus said to them, "Come ye yourselves apart into a desert place, and rest a while."

It would seem that, when the crowds saw them leave, they hurriedly made their way around the northern end of the Sea of Galilee. When Jesus and his disciples disembarked, there the people were by the thousands to meet them.

Outwardly Jesus had been thwarted in his purpose to be alone with the twelve. Yet, when he saw the multitudes he was moved, as always, not with anger but with deep and genuine compassion "because they were as sheep not having a shepherd" (v. 34). What would happen in this our day if we who follow Christ had the same genuine compassion for the lost and the needy that Jesus had?

1. *Feeding the Five Thousand* (6:35–44)

All through the day Jesus taught the people, and by late afternoon (v. 35) they were hungry. The disciples would have solved the problem by sending the crowds away. Jesus would not agree to such a thing.

John's Gospel tells us (John 6:7) that it was Philip who pointed out that it would take no less than two hundred pennyworth of bread to provide for such a multitude. The word "pennyworth" is a translation of the word *denarius*. A denarius was a day's wages for a working man. The disciples' resources, certainly, were all too meager to pay such a bill as that.

In reply to Philip, Jesus simply inquired as to how much food was available. At this, Andrew stepped forward to say that a lad in the crowd (John 6:8–9) had five barley loaves and two fishes, hardly enough to satisfy one hungry man.

Mark records that Jesus, taking in his hands this scant supply of food and looking up to heaven, blessed and brake the bread until at last there was enough for everyone, with twelve baskets full left over after the meal.

There has been much discussion as to the spiritual significance of this miracle. It should be remembered that Jesus' central purpose in this part of his public ministry was to train the twelve. While this miracle was the natural response of the loving heart of Jesus to human need, it was, at the same time, a fine opportunity for him to demonstrate to his disciples that, of a truth, there are no limits to the power of God. Besides this, the feeding of the five thousand carried a spiritual message for all who witnessed it and for all who would later hear of it. Jesus' miracles were often parables of teaching. It was a way of saying to the people, "I am the bread of life."

2. *Jesus Walking on the Sea* (6:45–52)

The people were greatly impressed with the feeding of the five thousand, so impressed, indeed, that they decided to acclaim Jesus the king of Israel (John 6:15). To meet this crisis, Jesus sent his disciples to Bethsaida, on the other side of the lake, and, when he had dispersed the people, he went alone "into a mountain to pray" (v. 46).

The "fourth watch of the night" (v. 48) was the three-hour period just before sunrise. So it was very early the next morning when Jesus arose and, looking out upon the lake, saw his disciples battling against a storm. Immediately, he went to their aid, walking out upon the waters. Oddly enough, the disciples did not recognize the Lord. They thought, rather, that they were seeing a ghost and were all the more afraid, until, across the waves, came a familiar voice saying, "Be of good cheer: it is I; be not afraid" (v. 50).

Here again is a miracle which seems to have no obvious

spiritual meaning and purpose until we look at it more closely. It was, first of all, the natural response of Jesus to human need. It was also another opportunity to teach the disciples a much-needed lesson. When things looked bad, the disciples invariably lost their courage and their faith. This would never do.

All too soon storms of persecution that were far more treacherous than the storms on the Sea of Galilee would threaten to engulf the disciples. They needed to be made aware of the abiding fact that divine help and divine companionship are ever available to the child of God. That they had not yet learned this lesson is made obvious by Mark's comment, "For they understood not concerning the loaves, but their heart was hardened" (v. 52 ASV).

3. *Return to Galilee* (6:53–56)

Upon returning to Gennesaret, in Galilee, Jesus was met again by crowds of people, some of whom "ran through that whole region" (v. 55) announcing his presence in their midst. As before, they came not to acknowledge him as their Lord but to seek healing for their bodies. They had discovered that only to touch the hem of his garment was to be made whole (v. 56).

4. *Ceremonial Defilement* (7:1–23)

It seems that the greater the acclaim of the people in general was for Jesus, the more determined the scribes and Pharisees were to discredit him. On this occasion they hit upon the fact that Jesus did not instruct nor encourage the disciples to observe the Jewish traditions concerning ceremonial cleanliness.

The tradition of the elders insisted that the Jews should wash their hands frequently, not simply as a matter of good health and physical cleanliness but to avoid ceremonial contamination by the Gentiles. This tradition was an attempt to apply to the people generally a law that was originally given for the priests in the handling of holy food.

In answering the scribes and the Pharisees, Jesus dealt first of all with their traditions in general, and then specifically with the matter of ceremonial cleansing. In making the point that the traditions of the elders had lost most, if not all, of their spiritual significance, Jesus referred to a practice among the Jewish people that had resulted in nothing short of sheer hypocrisy.

Their traditions declared that a man must put God first in the stewardship of his possessions. In itself, this was as it should have been. But the traditions ruled that a man could declare a certain portion of his wealth to be "Corban," that is, holy unto God. Usually the money was given to the priests for the Temple services.

As time went on, however, many people used this tradition as an excuse to avoid fulfilling their just obligations. Instead of caring for his aged parents as the laws of Moses required, a man would say, "I cannot afford to do this since I have designated my money as dedicated to God." In many cases, this claim was just a ruse, and the money was never given to the priests. In this fashion the leaders had nullified the law of God (the laws of Moses) by claiming to adhere to the traditions of the elders. In this they were no longer the servants of God, Jesus implied, but outright hypocrites (v. 6).

Turning then to the question of ceremonial defilement, Jesus set forth a spiritual principle that is as applicable to our own day as it was to the day in which it was uttered. He declared that defilement is not a physical matter; it is a matter of the heart. True religion is not ritual; it is righteousness. A man is spiritually clean only as he is clean in motive, in attitude, in thought. Is this not the very core of our Christian faith? It is in accord with the words of Jesus, "Except a man be born again, he cannot see the kingdom of God" (John 3:3). It was at this very point that Jesus and the Pharisees stood poles apart.

III. THE SECOND WITHDRAWAL (7:24–30)
(Cf. Matt. 15:21–28)

The clamor of the crowds, on the one hand, and the antipathy of the Pharisees, on the other, led Jesus to withdraw again from Galilee. This time he went into Phoenicia, which was Gentile territory, the people being descendants of the Canaanites. The two most significant cities in Phoenicia were Tyre and Sidon.

Once again, Jesus' presence soon became noised about and, in due time, a Syrophenician woman came beseeching him to heal her daughter of an unclean spirit. Jesus' immediate response to the woman has raised a great deal of discussion. Did he mean to rebuke her? Was there any possibility that her feelings were hurt by the blunt words, "For it is not meet to take the children's bread, and to cast it unto the dogs"? (v. 27).

We may explain that Jesus was simply quoting a well-known saying of that day and that, by the tone of his voice and the look in his eyes, the woman recognized the words to be spoken good-humoredly. This interpretation is borne out by the fact that she, rather adroitly, answered him with another current proverb and with equally good humor, as she replied, "Yes, Lord: yet the dogs under the table eat of the children's crumbs."

Perhaps an even better explanation is that, here again, Jesus was primarily interested in training the twelve, who at that very moment stood around him. He knew that what he first said exactly expressed the point of view that they, as Jews, had held through the years. As he spoke the words, they possibly nodded their assent as if to say, "That is just the way we see it."

58 A STUDY OF THE GOSPEL OF MARK

Then, by his miracle of healing at the Gentile woman's request, Jesus went on to show the disciples that henceforth it would not be so. While he, himself, was sent primarily to "the lost sheep of the house of Israel" (Matt. 15:24), the ministry of his message would at last be given to peoples of every race and nation. This incident, therefore, was in a very real sense a portent of the world mission of the gospel.

Jesus went on to say to the Gentile woman, "For this saying go thy way; the devil is gone out of thy daughter" (v. 29).

IV. WITHDRAWAL FROM PHOENICIA (7:31 to 8:12)
(Cf. Matt. 15:39 to 16:4)

There is no record as to how long Jesus remained in the region of Tyre and Sidon (Phoenicia). We may assume that the report of the healing of the Syrophenician girl quickly spread throughout the territory. Jesus was still intent upon being alone with the twelve. Therefore he decided to withdraw from Phoenicia, going to the region known as "the Decapolis," which lay on the east of the Jordan River and largely to the south of the Sea of Galilee. As he journeyed, he carefully avoided the territory that was governed by Herod Antipas.

1. *Cure of the Deaf Mute* (7:31–37)

As usual, Jesus was met by a multitude of people (v. 33) who brought with them a man who was both deaf and mute. Since Jesus' purpose at that moment was to be alone with his disciples, he took the man aside from the crowd to avoid publicity as much as possible.

The conduct of Jesus as he put his fingers in the man's ears and touched the man's tongue was unusual. It is perhaps best explained by the fact that Jesus accommodated his method of healing to the special needs of the particular individual. Since the man was both deaf and mute, the only way to communicate with him was by means of a sign language. This Jesus did by placing his fingers in the man's ears to signify that it was his purpose to restore the man's hearing, and by moistening the man's tongue to indicate the purpose, also, to restore his speech.

Over and over again, we read that Jesus instructed those whom he healed (and sometimes even his own disciples) not to publish the matter abroad. The reason for this instruction, of course, was that he was anxious not to add fuel to the fires of popular acclaim that were already raging too fiercely. He desired to use his time, as much as possible, in the instruction of the twelve.

2. *Feeding the Four Thousand* (8:1-9)

In spite of Jesus' injunction to the contrary, the news of the cure of the deaf-mute was widely publicized, with the result that some four thousand people crowded around Jesus. For three days they waited upon the ministry of his words. From sheer compassion (v. 3), he decided to feed them. This miracle has, at times, been confused with the feeding of the five thousand. According to Jesus' own words, as recorded by Mark, (8:19-20), they were two separate miracles. The details of the two miracles differ but the significance of them is identical. For the crowds, they were miracles of compassion and instruction. For the twelve, they were miracles of instruction.

3. *Brief Visit to Galilee* (8:10-12)

It became quite obvious that Jesus would find no privacy or respite in the Decapolis, so again he and his disciples crossed the lake to Dalmanutha, or Magadan. Hardly had they disembarked, it would seem, than the Pharisees came to harass Jesus. This time they did not enter into a controversy with him. Perhaps they had already learned that they were no match for him in an argument. Instead, they asked for "a sign from heaven." (v. 11). By this they apparently meant some mighty demonstration, such as a finger writing in the skies proclaiming him to be the Messiah—some sign that everyone could see. Jesus well knew that their request was insincere, so he flatly denied it without a further word.

V. THE FOURTH WITHDRAWAL (8:13 to 9:29)
(Cf. Matt. 16:5 to 17:20; Luke 9:18–43)

Once again Jesus attempted to be alone with his disciples. This time he was more successful. Except for two instances—one recorded at the beginning of this section of Mark's gospel, and one at the end of it—the crowds were not present. At last, Jesus had the opportunity to face the twelve with certain matters concerning his messiahship and his saving ministry. About these matters they must be made quite certain before they could be ready to face the hour of their Lord's crucifixion. Together, Jesus and the twelve set out across the lake for the regions of Caesarea Philippi.

1. *Warning Against the Doctrine of the Pharisees* (8:13–21)

On the way across the lake, Jesus was apparently still thinking of his recent clash with the Pharisees. He was keenly aware of their entrenched opposition. He knew how to handle them, but would his disciples be equally adept in the days ahead? One of the worst things that could happen to his cause in those beginning days would be for his disciples to compromise with the religious authorities and particularly with the Pharisees, whose way of life was altogether different from the way of life that Jesus taught. It was possibly with some such thoughts as these in mind that he said to his disciples, in effect: "Guard against the Pharisees. They will attempt to nullify everything you try to do."

The response of the disciples indicated that they still had a great deal to learn, for they missed the point of Jesus' warning entirely. They thought, rather, that he was talking about bread, for the term leaven was commonly so used. Jesus upbraided them for their lack of perception. If he had been speaking simply of bread, why would that be any matter of concern? Had he not supplied bread once for five thousand and, again, for four thousand? It would be an easy matter to take care of their meager needs.

To make clear his disappointment in them, Jesus went on to say: "How is it that ye do not understand?" (v. 21). Matthew points out that only then did his disciples realize that Jesus was referring to "the doctrine of the Pharisees and of the Sadducees" (Matt. 16:12).

2. *The Blind Man at Bethsaida* (8:22-26)

Arriving at Bethsaida, Jesus was met by a group of people who brought a blind man with them. As in the case of the deaf-mute (7:31-37), Jesus used an unusual procedure in healing the blind man. It seems that there was a prevailing tradition in those days to the effect that saliva had certain healing qualities. It may very well be that the use of saliva in this particular miracle strengthened the man's faith. This is the only recorded miracle where the healing was gradual and progressive. Here again, we may assume that the method was employed solely for the sake of the man himself, though there are some commentators who see in it a parable of the progressive nature of our Christian experience.

3. *The Great Confession* (8:27-33)

At long last Jesus gained the objective for which he had sought—to be all alone with the twelve. He must now prepare them for the trying experiences that were in store for them. But first there was one all-important thing that he must know. Did they fully accept him as the promised Deliverer? To be sure, he knew their hearts. Yet he wanted to hear from their own lips that they assuredly knew his true identity—his relationship with the Father, his purpose in his earthly mission. So he asked them, almost abruptly: "Who do men say that I am?" (v. 27 ASV). This was not the main question, but it would set them to thinking.

One after another they began to recall what the people had said about Jesus. Some had identified him with John the Baptist, others with Elijah or with various other prophets. Then came the acid test: "But who say ye that I am?" (v. 29 ASV).

It was Peter who answered, for himself and the others, with the clear and unqualified confession, "Thou art the Christ" (v. 29). That confession was what Jesus wanted to hear. The disciples were now ready for him to tell them, in no uncertain terms, what lay before him, and them, in Jerusalem (v. 31).

While Peter was quite sincere in his confession, the implications of Jesus' messiahship were more than he could bear. Peter began to rebuke Jesus. He believed that Jesus was the Messiah, but he could not see why that should mean Jesus' death in Jerusalem at the hands of the religious leaders. A short while before, Jesus had praised Peter; now he rebuked him. Peter, who had acted like a veritable rock, was now acting like Satan, making the same sort of a proposal that Satan had made during the temptation in the wilderness —the proposal that Jesus avoid the cross.

4. *The Way of Discipleship* (8:34 to 9:1)

Jesus went on to declare that not only was his way the way of the cross but so, also, was the way of every one who followed in his steps. He was willing to die for the cause to which he had set himself. They also must be willing to die, if need be, for their Master's sake and for the sake of the gospel. Jesus then amplified this truth in three further statements, saying in effect, "It is a poor bargain if a man shall seek to save his life at the cost of his own soul." One wonders whether Peter recalled these words later when he denied Christ.

The solemn words of Jesus are spoken just as directly to those of us who claim to follow him in this day as they were to the disciples long ago. The way of the Christian is the way of the cross.

Jesus' final word to his disciples at this point was a declaration that the day of which he spoke was not far off. Some of them would actually see the kingdom of God coming in power. They would see Jesus fulfil his messianic mission in his death upon the cross (9:1).

5. *The Transfiguration* (9:2-8)

About a week later, Jesus, desiring to prepare his disciples further for the coming events, took Peter, James, and John up into a high mountain. There he was transfigured before them. "And there appeared unto them Elias with Moses: and they were talking with Jesus" (v. 4).

In the midst of this transfiguration, Peter simply could not remain silent. Hardly knowing just what to say, he declared in effect: "This is all so wonderful! Why can't we build three tabernacles and remain up here, far from the troublesome crowd?"

Perhaps Peter was remembering the sufferings that awaited them in Jerusalem and felt that this would be a convenient way of avoiding that dark hour. But Peter was speaking out of turn. The pageant of the transfiguration was not yet over for, in a moment, they heard a voice from out of the clouds saying, "This is my beloved Son: hear him" (v. 7).

Someone has said that this proclamation from heaven had the same significance for the disciples that a similar announcement had for John the Baptist by the river Jordan. It was the seal and sign of God's approval upon Jesus as the Messiah, the Saviour of mankind. The appearance of Moses and Elijah with Jesus implied that the purpose of God in the law (Moses) and the prophets (Elijah) had found its fulfilment in the gospel (Jesus).

6. A Question About Elijah (9:9–13)

The experience on the mountain was too much for the three disciples. On the way down they conversed with Jesus, who suggested that they keep silent about the transfiguration until "the Son of man were risen from the dead" (v. 9).

Reference to the resurrection brought up another question: What did Jesus mean? Possibly, the name of Elijah (who had appeared on the Mount of Transfiguration) was mentioned. This led to another question. Was it not commonly believed that Elijah would appear before the advent of the Messiah? Had he appeared? Yes, said Jesus, he had appeared, and he had fared ill at the hands of his enemies. Apparently Jesus was implying that John the Baptist had fulfilled the prophetic role of Elijah and that he himself would receive no better treatment than John the Baptist had received.

7. The Powerless Disciples (9:14–29)

Soon Jesus and the three came upon the remaining nine disciples in the midst of a heated discussion. It turned out that a man had brought his boy with an unclean spirit to the disciples, beseeching them that they heal him. They had been powerless to do the boy any good, and their powerlessness had raised no little questioning among the bystanders as to whether, after all, they really had the gifts that had been so widely attributed to them.

It would seem that Jesus addressed his words of rebuke (v. 19) not only to the nine disciples but also to the crowd and especially, perhaps, to the scribes who were making capital out of the disciples' failure. Then he turned to the father of the boy and began to inquire as to the history of the boy's illness. The father was only too willing to tell Jesus the boy's story, and concluded by saying, "But if thou canst do any thing, have compassion on us, and help us" (v. 22).

To this, Jesus responded, "If thou canst believe, all things are possible to him that believeth" (v. 23). There is a note of pathos in the father's further reply. In effect he said: "I believe but my faith is weak. Give me the power to have a stronger faith." At this, Jesus released the boy from the power of the evil spirit.

The nine disciples were frankly embarrassed. Why had they failed so miserably? Jesus' answer gave them little room for comfort for he plainly told them that they could do mighty works only after much prayer. Is it not equally true that our powerlessness as the followers of Jesus Christ is often due to our prayerlessness?

SUGGESTIONS FOR STUDY AND DISCUSSION

1. On a map of Palestine, trace the journeying of Jesus during this period of his ministry. If possible secure a small map for your notebook.

2. In a good Bible dictionary (Harper's *Bible Dictionary* is recommended) read the article on the family of Herod the Great and make out a chart for your notebook that will show the relationship between Herodias, Herod Antipas, and Salome.

3. Read this section of Mark's Gospel (6:14 to 9:29) in one sitting and then make out your own outline for your notebook.

4. In a harmony of the Gospels (*A Harmony of the Gospels* by A. T. Robertson, is recommended) compare the passages in the other three Gospels that deal with the same period in the life of Jesus as that covered by Mark 6:14 to 9:29.

CHAPTER 5

I. A BRIEF VISIT TO GALILEE (9:30–50)
   1. Concerning His Death and Resurrection (vv. 30–32)
   2. Concerning True Greatness (vv. 33–35)
   3. A Pertinent Illustration (vv. 36–37)
   4. Concerning Tolerance (vv. 38–40)
   5. Concerning Hindrances (vv. 41–48)
   6. Self-discipline and the Christian Witness (vv. 49–50)

II. BEYOND THE JORDAN (10:1–31)
   1. Teaching Concerning Divorce (vv. 1–12)
   2. Teaching Concerning Children (vv. 13–16)
   3. Teaching Concerning Wealth (vv. 17–27)
   4. Teaching Concerning Sacrifice and Rewards (vv. 28–31)

III. NEARING JERUSALEM (10:32–52)
   1. Third Prediction of His Death and Resurrection (vv. 33–34)
   2. The Request of James and John (vv. 35–45)
   3. Blind Bartimeus (vv. 46–52)

5

MOVING TOWARD JERUSALEM

Mark 9:30 to 10:52

THE GREAT CONFESSION of Peter and the ensuing transfiguration have been called "the watershed in the public ministry of Jesus." From that time forward, the shadows of the cross lay continually across his pathway. More than ever, his primary concern was to prepare the twelve for the crisis which lay ahead. From this point in Mark's story, therefore, less notice is given to Jesus' ministry of healing, and more attention is focused on his teaching ministry. Less mention is made of the attending multitudes, and more emphasis is placed upon Jesus' relationship to his disciples.

I. A BRIEF VISIT TO GALILEE (9:30–50)
(Cf. Matt. 17:22 to 18:14; Luke 9:43–50)

Leaving the Decapolis, with his disciples Jesus went first to Galilee. Mark observes that Jesus was careful not to allow his presence in Galilee to become widely known (v. 30)— partly because of his desire to concentrate upon the training of the twelve; partly because of Herod's growing antipathy; and partly, perhaps, because of the increasing bitterness of the scribes and Pharisees toward him.

1. *Concerning His Death and Resurrection* (vv. 30–32)

It would seem that Mark is attempting to summarize Jesus' central message to the disciples during this particular period, as he writes: "For he taught his disciples, and said unto them,

The Son of man is delivered into the hands of men, and they shall kill him; and after that he is killed, he shall rise the third day" (v. 31). Over and over again Jesus spoke to his disciples of his death and resurrection.

It is quite evident that, while the disciples believed that Jesus was, indeed, the promised Deliverer, they continued to envision a victorious Messiah who would destroy his enemies and set up a temporal kingdom. Jesus sought to rectify this misconception. This accounts for his apparent bluntness in referring to his coming death, "They shall kill him." Surely he could not put it more clearly than that. He was not at this time going to destroy his enemies with a vast show of power. On the contrary, they were going to seek to destroy him. The disciples understood his words but they did not understand the meaning of those words.

In this connection Jesus used a title which he applied to himself quite often, "the Son of man." This title occurs fourteen times in Mark's Gospel. Some students of the Bible see it as a reference to the humanity of Jesus. According to this view, Jesus was emphasizing the fact that, although he was the Son of God, he was also the Son of man and, as a man, he would be subjected by his enemies to all manner of human suffering and even to death.

Other students see in this title an acknowledgment of Jesus' messiahship. The term was used by the prophet Daniel to describe one who would descend from heaven to preside over the last judgment and the new age (Dan. 7:13). If this interpretation is the correct one, then Jesus was looking beyond his death and resurrection to his coming again in clouds of glory.

Certainly, the disciples did not grasp any such implication as this. Perhaps, they had at last come to realize that, in some way or another, dark days lay ahead of them, but they did not hold any assurance of their Lord's resurrection. It was a concept which, at that moment, was far too great for them.

2. *Concerning True Greatness* (vv. 33–35)

That the twelve did not grasp the real significance of Jesus' messianic mission, that they did not understand that his kingdom was a spiritual kingdom and not a temporal one, is borne out by their conversation on the way to Capernaum. They had apparently been arguing one with another as to which of them would hold the highest rank in the coming kingdom. It is quite possible that Peter and James and John, remembering that they had been singled out by Jesus to go with him on the Mount of Transfiguration, felt that they stood in line for the chief honors.

It should, however, be said in defense of the disciples that, while they argued about places of greatness in the kingdom, they were not willing for Jesus to know about it. When he questioned them about their conversation, they were too ashamed to answer him. Evidently they knew in their hearts that self-seeking and selfish ambition did not fit in at all with what Jesus had said to them from time to time.

Jesus assumed the typical posture of a teacher of that day as he sat down in their midst and called the twelve around him. He gave them a frank lesson on the true nature of greatness in the kingdom of God. It was a hard lesson for them to learn, even as it is a hard lesson for us. The teaching of Jesus stands out in sharp contrast with the standards of the world.

The worldly standard declares: "Work diligently to attain the topmost rung of the ladder of success. Never be satisfied until you are the most competent, or the richest, or the most famous man in your field." Jesus taught: "If any man desire to be first, the same shall be last of all, and servant of all" (v. 35).

It should be clearly understood that Jesus did not decry

ambition. He did not say that a man should not seek to be great. What he did say was that, if a man desired greatness, he should seek to reach his goal, not by serving his own interests, but by rendering service to others. In a way, the world at large has acknowledged the validity of this principle. The men and women of almost every generation who have been most highly esteemed have not been those who have done much to help themselves and to advance their own cause. They have been those who have done much for the sake of others. It is incumbent upon every devout Christian, constantly to ask himself not, "What gain may I accrue for myself?" but, "What good may I do for others, for Christ's sake?"

3. *A Pertinent Illustration* (vv. 36-37)

To enforce his teaching, Jesus beckoned a little child who was in the home where they were staying and, taking the child in his arms, he said to the disciples, "Whosoever shall receive one of such children in my name, receiveth me: and whosoever shall receive me, receiveth not me, but him that sent me" (v. 37).

Jesus was illustrating the timeless truth that he was trying to teach his disciples. He was not simply saying that they should be kind to little children, though that is involved. He was saying that his followers must be willing to render service to any individual, even though there is little possibility that such an individual can in any way repay that kindness. We manifest kindness to a little child, not with thought of reward, but because we instinctively love little children and wish to be of help to them. This is the attitude that the servant of Christ should have to all who are weak, or helpless, or in need. When we habitually take such an attitude towards the "little people" of the world because of our relationship to Jesus Christ (in Jesus' name) we render service to Jesus Christ and to God.

4. *Concerning Tolerance* (vv. 38-40)

The idea of being helpful in Jesus' name recalled a recent incident to John's mind. He and his fellow disciples had seen an unknown man casting out demons in Jesus' name. Instead of being helpful to the man, they had spoken quite roughly to him. John was, therefore, saying in effect, to Jesus, "Do you mean that we did wrong in rebuking that man?"

Jesus replied "Forbid him not. . . . For he that is not against us is for us" (vv. 39-40 ASV).

The lesson on tolerance was a difficult one for the twelve to learn. It is no less difficult for us. All of us, surely, believe in freedom of thought and freedom of expression. But how hard it is to feel friendly towards those who differ from us in national tradition or political viewpoint or religious conviction! This teaching does not mean that we are, under any circumstance, to compromise our convictions. It means that we must try to respect the convictions that others hold, even though we do not see things their way. It means that we must accord to every man the right to think for himself and to speak for himself.

A great philosopher once said to those who violently opposed him, "I do not agree with a word that you say but I will defend, to the death, your right to say it." This is tolerance.

5. *Concerning Hindrances* (vv. 41-48)

Jesus pointed out that the man who was casting out demons was actually rendering service to mankind, in spite of the fact that he was not a member of the group of immediate followers. This circumstance led Jesus to declare that any service that is rendered in his name will be rewarded, even to the giving of a cup of cold water, little as that may be. By the same token, any disservice we render our fellow man will earn God's disapproval. For a disciple of Christ to be a hindrance to anyone, no matter how insignificant that individual may be, is a sin—so grave a sin that "it is better for him that a millstone were hanged about his neck, and he were cast into the sea" (v. 42).

Having warned his disciples about being a hindrance to others, Jesus spoke about dealing with hindrances in their own lives. Just as it is necessary, at times, for a man to have a hand, or a foot, or an eye amputated to prevent infection from spreading throughout his entire body, so it is necessary, always, to get rid of anything in one's heart or mind that prevents complete devotion to God. Anything in the life of a disciple that is unseemly or improper must be eliminated by the grace of God.

J. Henry Jowett once said, "No man ever took his besetting sin and, as it were, 'cut it out' without, thereby, receiving new strength of character." [1]

How sobering are these words of Jesus! "It is better for thee to enter halt into life, than having two feet to be cast into hell, into the fire that never shall be quenched: where their worm dieth not, and the fire is not quenched" (vv. 45–46). Surely, "the wages of sin is death" (Rom. 6:23).

6. *Self-discipline and the Christian Witness* (vv. 49–50)

As the disciples listened to Jesus, they were possibly saying within themselves, "How hard it is to enter into the kingdom!" Jesus consented to their thoughts as he further said that to be a faithful follower of his meant to exercise rigorous self-discipline. He had just mentioned the judgment of sin in no uncertain terms. He spoke next of purification from sin as he said, "For every one shall be salted with fire" (v. 49). Purification of thought and purpose and motive is essential if the servants of Christ would, in turn, have a wholesome and redemptive effect upon the world around them. Unless the Christian is purged from sin, he is like salt without savor; his witness is ineffective.

This passage in Mark's Gospel recalls the words of Jesus in the Sermon on the Mount: "Ye are the salt of the earth" (Matt. 5:13). To fulfil our ministry as Christ's agents of redemption in the world, we must be wholly dedicated to the Lord. Jesus concluded his discourse concerning true greatness by saying that the disciples could not be the salt of the earth unless harmony prevailed in the fellowship (v. 50).

II. BEYOND THE JORDAN (10:1–31)
(Cf. Matt. 19:1 to 20:16; Luke 18:15–30)

At this point in Mark's story, Jesus left Galilee for the last time, on his journey to Jerusalem and the cross.

1. *Teaching Concerning Divorce* (vv. 1–12)

On the way, the crowds again gathered around the Lord and, as was his custom, "he taught them again" (v. 1). In due course, the Pharisees approached him with a question that was quite controversial in those days—the question of divorce. Amongst the religious leaders there were two schools of thought on this subject.

The discussion revolved around Deuteronomy 24:1: "When a man taketh a wife, and marrieth her, then it shall be, if she find no favor in his eyes, because he hath found some unseemly thing in her, that he shall write her a bill of divorcement, and give it in her hand, and send her out of his house" (ASV).

The point of contention was as to what Moses meant by "some unseemly thing." The followers of the teacher Shammai held that a wife could not be divorced except for unfaithfulness. The disciples of Hillel, on the other hand, held to a much broader interpretation and permitted divorce for almost any cause (Matt. 19:3). As a result of this more liberal interpretation, the divorce situation among the Jews in Jesus' day was deplorable, falling far short of the divine standards set forth in the Old Testament and taking on characteristics of the customs of surrounding peoples. As one student of Jewish life puts it:

> Jewish society was disgraced by an appalling laxity in the matter of divorce. Family life was imperilled by it and an intolerable wrong was done to womanhood. It made woman the slave of man, putting the wife at the husband's mercy. For, while she could not for any cause divorce him, he might, for no cause at all, divorce her and cast her out upon the world.[2]

It is difficult to determine the motive of the Pharisees in presenting this burning issue of the day to Jesus. Certainly they were not sincere in their approach to him because they came "tempting him" (v. 2). Perhaps they desired to set Jesus at odds with a large segment of the Jewish leadership since, whatever side of the question he took, his position would be violently opposed by the representatives of the other side. It may have been that the Pharisees knew only too well where Jesus would stand and they wanted to report that he had no respect for the laws of Moses.

Whatever the true purpose of his questioners, Jesus did not dodge the issue. He began his answer by saying that Moses' law was an improvement over the prevailing practice before Moses' day. That practice permitted a man to divorce his wife without having to specify the cause for the divorce. Then Jesus went on to declare that, in the sight of God, marriage is an inviolable union. It is a part of the divine scheme of things that a man shall "leave his father and mother, and shall cleave [be joined] to his wife; and the two shall become one. . . . What therefore God hath joined together, let not man put asunder" (vv. 7–9 ASV).

Jesus' statement is the Christian concept of marriage. It is a concept that should be held clearly in mind by all who enter into this sacred union. As someone has phrased it, "Marriage is for keeps." A man and a woman enter into a sacred and lasting contract when they solemnly promise "to have and to hold" each other "until death do us part."

In Mark's record of this incident, Jesus' answer to the Pharisees ends at this point. Later, when he was alone with his disciples, they asked him further about the matter and he said to them: "Whosoever shall put away his wife, and marry another, committeth adultery against her. And if a woman shall put away her husband, and be married to another, she committeth adultery" (vv. 11-12). This is a sweeping statement. Are there no grounds for divorce?

Mark was concerned with the Christian ideal of marriage as Jesus stated it to the disciples in the house later on. The Christian ideal is that both parties will remain faithful to their marriage vows, making divorce out of the question. This is how it ought to be.

The problem of divorce is as vexing in our day as it was in Jesus' day. It has been said repeatedly that in the United States one out of three marriages ends in divorce. There is certainly need for a quickening of the Christian conscience at this point. Parents may render invaluable service by interpreting to their children the Christian ideal of marriage as a lasting union. Ministers have a responsibility to impress upon those who present themselves for marriage the permanence of the relationship into which they are about to enter.

2. *Teaching Concerning Children* (vv. 13-16)

When a group of parents came bringing their little children to Jesus to receive his blessing, the disciples objected strenuously and evidently quite rudely. Jesus was too busy to be bothered with parents and their children, they reasoned. However, the disciples did not understand the spirit of their Master. Jesus seems always to have had time for those who sought his help and blessing, no matter how pressing the affairs of the moment were.

Jesus was genuinely displeased with his disciples for their brusqueness and impatience. In response, he uttered words that have been cherished by young and old alike through the years, as, taking the children in his arms and laying his hands upon them (v. 16), he said, "Suffer [permit] the little children to come unto me; forbid them not: for to such belongeth the kingdom of God" (v. 14 ASV).

These words of Jesus mean that all who enter the kingdom of God must have the receptiveness, the simple trust, the sense of dependence, and the sense of helplessness that characterize a child.

> Unless we are prepared to receive God's Kingdom (or salvation) as a child receives a gift at his father's hand, we shall not have it. It is a parable of pure grace. And men still receive God's Kingdom as little children. The Kingdom of our Father is not for the proud and self-sufficient but for those who, owning their weakness, cast themselves on God's grace and mercy made available for them in Christ.[3]

The phrase "forbid them not," or "do not hinder them" gives all of us concern. It is all too easy to discourage children from making Christ the Lord of their lives. We may discourage them by failing to show the fruit of the Spirit in our lives, by failing to give proper place to prayer and the reading of the Bible in the home, by manifesting little or no interest in the services of the church, or by doing things that we would not want the children to do. In the light of Jesus' words, the responsibility of parenthood is a serious matter. Indeed, the responsibility of all adults in this respect is a serious matter, for we never know when some little child is walking in our footsteps.

3. *Teaching Concerning Wealth* (vv. 17–27)

Again, on the road to Jerusalem, Jesus was met by a young man who ran excitedly to him and reverently knelt at his feet saying, "Good Master, what shall I do that I may inherit eternal life?" (v. 17).

How it must have warmed our Lord's heart to hear these words so earnestly spoken! This was precisely the question he longed to hear from the lips of men. To test the depth of the man's sincerity he bluntly asked him, "Why callest thou me good? there is none good but one, that is, God" (v. 18). In other words, he asked him frankly, "Do you really believe that I am God?" The young man had no answer to that question, so Jesus probed him still further to discover what effort he had thus far made to enter the kingdom.

Without a moment's hesitation, the man replied: "Master, all these have I observed from my youth" (v. 20). He had habitually made it a practice to keep the commandments, to do no evil, but that was not enough. With all of his wealth, what good had he done? It would appear that he had done very little positive good. He loved his wealth for its own sake and not for the sake of the means it afforded him to serve others. This was his central problem. He must find victory at this point or he could not follow Jesus.

The words of the rich young ruler find echo in the words of the apostle Paul, written some years later. He too had been blameless as "touching the righteousness which is in the law" (Phil. 3:6). Paul, however, had taken the step which the rich young ruler was not willing to take. He had come to the place where he could truthfully say, "But what things were gain to me, those I counted loss for Christ" (Phil. 3:7).

A man does not become a Christian by using his natural resources to help others. He does, however, become a Christian when he reaches the place where he is willing to give up anything that stands between him and Christ, whether it be wealth, or pleasure, or ambition, or self-indulgence, or any other thing.

At the words, "Go, sell whatsoever thou hast, and give to the poor, and thou shalt have treasure in heaven: and come, follow me" (v. 21 ASV), the young ruler decided that the price was too great. Having come to Jesus full of excitement and enthusiasm, he went away full of sadness. Jesus, too, was saddened, for he saw great possibilities in the young man. Turning to his disciples, he warned them that it was not easy to put God first in one's life, especially when it meant the making of a genuine sacrifice. How hard it is for a man of ample means to feel dependent upon God! And yet, a man who trusts in his own resources simply cannot enter into the kingdom (vv. 24–25).

4. *Teaching Concerning Sacrifice and Rewards* (vv. 28–31)

The saying of Jesus concerning wealth greatly troubled the disciples. They still hoped that Jesus would set up an earthly kingdom and that they would share in its prestige and resources. Peter's statement, "Lo, we have left all, and have followed thee" (v. 28), indicates that the disciples were looking forward to a material reward for their faithfulness. Not so, said Jesus.

To be sure, there would be rewards for leaving "house, or brethren, or sisters, or father, or mother, or wife, or children, or lands, for my sake, and the gospel's" (v. 29). They would not be material rewards; they would be the rewards of a larger relationship with all who followed in the way of Christ, a kinship with the entire family of God in this world, and, at last, the greatest reward of all—eternal life (v. 30). Many who have most now may have least in the hereafter, and many who do not rank high in this life will be greatly rewarded in the life to come (v. 31).

III. Nearing Jerusalem (10:32–52)
(Cf. Matt. 20:17–34; Luke 18:31–43)

Mark now describes what was undoubtedly a tense and dramatic moment in the journey of Jesus to Jerusalem. Apparently, as they neared the city, Jesus suddenly stepped out ahead of them with a strange look in his eyes and a sense of purpose and determination in his bearing. His manner caused the disciples to feel that something momentous was about to happen. The word that is here translated "amazed" really means "terrified." It would seem that fear spread throughout the entire group that was following Jesus.

1. *Third Prediction of His Death and Resurrection* (vv. 33–34)

Jesus did not attempt to allay their fears. He did not minimize the gravity of the situation into which they were moving. Instead, he again put in clear and simple language the truth about his impending death at the hands of the religious leaders in Jerusalem. On this occasion he went more into detail and described not only the suffering that awaited him but the shame that would be heaped upon him as he said, concerning himself: "And they shall mock him, and shall scourge him, and shall spit upon him, and shall kill him: and the third day he shall rise again" (v. 34). What a vivid picture of the events as they were actually to take place!

It should be noted that each time Jesus referred to his suffering and death (see 8:31; 9:31) he invariably concluded with mention of his resurrection on the third day. While he was fully aware of the travail that awaited him, he was ever mindful that the victory of his enemies would be short-lived. Beyond the pain of death lay the certainty of the resurrection. By itself, the cross is a gigantic tragedy. Coupled with the resurrection, it is the door of hope for all mankind.

2. *The Request of James and John* (vv. 35–45)

One would think that the disciples, upon hearing their Master's sobering words, would have been filled with compassionate concern for him. How dark was the way that lay before him! Yet, their thoughts were not for him but for themselves and their own advancement and prestige. They could not get away from the belief that Jesus would in the near future reign upon the earth as the Messiah, the second David. So, once again, just as they had done at the last time he spoke to them of his death and resurrection (9:31), they brought up the question of their places of honor in the kingdom.

It was James and John who brought up the subject. Without any apparent sense of impropriety they asked, "Grant unto us that we may sit, one on thy right hand, and the other on thy left hand, in thy glory" (v. 37). This request envisioned Jesus sitting on the throne of his kingdom with his ministers of state gathered about him, the chief minister sitting on his right and the minister next in rank on his left.

Jesus did not try to correct the incomplete understanding the disciples held concerning the nature of his kingdom. That problem would shortly be resolved. All too soon, they would discover just how mistaken they were. What Jesus did assail was their false notion of greatness in the kingdom. He had already clearly expressed himself on this subject (9:35) but, obviously, his words had fallen upon dull ears. James and John had used the imagery of the Gentile courts in which honors were handed out on the basis of favoritism and to gain political support. It would not be so in the kingdom of heaven. The honors of the kingdom are not gifts but rewards.

Chrysostom, one of the early church fathers, illustrated this quite well when he wrote:

> Let us suppose that there is an umpire, and many athletes enter the lists. Two of the athletes, who are very intimate with the umpire approach him and say, "Cause us to be crowned and proclaimed victors," on the strength of the goodwill and the friendship betwixt them." But he says to them, "This is not mine to give but is for them for whom it has been prepared by their efforts and sweat."[4]

Once again, Jesus set forth the Christian principle of greatness: "And whosoever of you will be the chiefest, shall be servant of all" (v. 44). On a previous occasion he had illustrated this principle by pointing to a little child (9:36). On this occasion, he illustrated it by referring to himself and his own sacrificial ministry. Even he, the Son of man, the promised Deliverer, came not to be served but to be a servant to the extent that he would, at last, yield up his life "a ransom for many" (v. 45).

The meaning of the phrase "a ransom for many," as applied to the death of Jesus Christ cannot better be defined than by a reference from the Old Testament: "But he was wounded for our transgressions, he was bruised for our iniquities: the chastisement of our peace was upon him; and with his stripes we are healed" (Isa. 53:5).

3. *Blind Bartimeus* (vv. 46–52)

The crowds journeying from Galilee to Jerusalem for the Passover usually avoided passing through despised Samaria by crossing the Jordan, making their way down the east side of the river, even as Jesus and his disciples had done. At Jericho, some fifteen miles from Jerusalem, the Passover pilgrims would recross the Jordan.

It was the custom for the people who, for one reason or another, could not attend the Passover to line the streets of Jericho to greet the passers-by. For this reason, the city was crowded when Jesus put in his appearance. Already the news of his coming had been widely heralded. There had been no little talk of his mighty miracles and his matchless teaching. Was this, indeed, the Messiah of promise? The atmosphere was tense with excitement. (The story of Zaccheus— Luke 19:1–10—belongs to this same period.)

As Jesus went out from Jericho, he came upon a blind man who was begging alms by the side of the road. Suddenly the man sensed the excitement that was in the air and asked what was going on. The answer was that Jesus of Nazareth was passing by. Immediately, blind Bartimeus began to cry out, not for alms but for healing. He would not be silenced by the crowd but persisted in crying, at the top of his voice, "Thou son of David, have mercy on me" (v. 48).

In the midst of all the tumult, Jesus heard the blind man's cry and spoke, "Call ye him." The many in the company who had sought to rebuke the earnest seeker were silenced by Jesus' words. Others, probably more friendly to Bartimeus, passed on the word: "Be of good comfort, rise, he calleth thee." Why did Bartimeus throw aside his cloak? Was not this an unusual act for a blind person, who would ordinarily be careful to keep his garments within reach? It may be that he expected to be able to see it when he turned back. Jesus, granting him his request said simply, "Go thy way; thy faith hath made thee whole" (v. 52).

The heart-warming note about this story is that, having recovered his sight, Bartimeus did not go off about his own business, but straightway joined the group who "followed Jesus in the way" (v. 52).

SUGGESTIONS FOR STUDY AND DISCUSSION

1. In your notebook write down some of the most significant teachings of Jesus on the Christian way of life as recorded in this section of Mark's Gospel. Discuss these teachings in class. To what extent do Christians generally put these teachings into practice?

2. Discuss Jesus' attitude toward little children. What is the significance of this for Christians today? What is meant by Jesus' words in Mark 10:14?

3. Discuss Jesus' teaching concerning tolerance. Name some instances in our own day where Christian tolerance needs to be manifested. The class may collect articles from current magazines and newspapers to illustrate situations in which Christian tolerance is needed.

4. Discuss the Christian attitude toward wealth. What did Jesus

mean when he said: "How hardly shall they that have riches enter into the kingdom of God!" (10:23)?

5. Make your own outline of this section of Mark's Gospel in your notebook.

---

[1] Benjamin Jowett, *The Speaker's Bible* (Aberdeen, Scotland: Speaker's Bible Office, 1948), p. 98.

[2] E. T. Thompson, *The Gospel According to Mark* (Richmond: John Knox Press, 1954), p. 161. Used by permission.

[3] Archibald M. Hunter, *The Gospel According to Saint Mark* (New York: The Macmillan Company, 1948), p. 101.

[4] David Smith, *In the Days of His Flesh* (New York: Harper & Brothers, 8th ed.), p. 380.

CHAPTER 6

I. THE TRIUMPHAL ENTRY (11:1–11)
II. THE WITHERED FIG TREE (11:12–14)
III. CLEANSING THE TEMPLE (11:15–19)
IV. A LESSON IN FAITH AND PRAYER (11:20–26)
V. CONFLICT WITH THE RELIGIOUS LEADERS (11:27 to 12:40)
   1. The Authority of Jesus (11:27–33)
   2. An Indictment of the Religious Leaders (12:1–12)
   3. A Question About Tribute (12:13–17)
   4. Concerning the Resurrection (12:18–27)
   5. The Question of a Scribe (12:28–34)
   6. Rebuking the Scribes (12:35–40)
VI. THE WIDOW'S MITE (12:41–44)

6

LAST PUBLIC MINISTRY IN JERUSALEM

Mark 11:1 to 12:44

THROUGHOUT OUR STUDY of Mark's Gospel, we have had occasion to notice that Jesus was continually aware of the dark and difficult days that lay before him and his disciples, in Jerusalem. Time and again, however, he carefully avoided forcing the issue "for his time had not yet come." He had much to do by way of proclaiming the new way of life that he had come to make possible for all who would believe in him. Especially was he anxious to instruct the twelve in preparation for the work which he would eventually put in their hands.

Now the hour had drawn near. With grim determination, Jesus steadfastly set his face toward Jerusalem. It was the season of the Passover. The city was filled with pilgrims from all the regions of Jerusalem and beyond. His earthly ministry was drawing to a close. No longer would he evade the opposition of the religious leaders. No longer would he urge those who proclaimed him as the promised Deliverer to hold their peace. He was ready to meet the opposition "head on."

I. THE TRIUMPHAL ENTRY (11:1–11)

(Cf. Matt. 21:1–11, 14–17; Luke 19:29–44; John 12:12–19)

There was an air of expectancy in Jerusalem at this time. The news had been noised abroad that the Deliverer was at hand. John tells us in his Gospel that the raising of Lazarus from the dead had made a terrific impression upon the people (John 12:9). The curious crowds, hearing that Jesus was on his way to the holy city, went out to meet him.

It would appear that Jesus had a threefold purpose in making a dramatic entrance into the city at that time. First, he desired openly to acknowledge the messianic tributes that had been offered him from time to time throughout his public ministry. One writer has said:

> The reason he did not silence the people who so acclaimed him, as hitherto he had never failed to do, is not hard to understand. He could not do so before without inviting misunderstanding and threatening his ministry. But now, the hour of decision has arrived. To conceal his claim any longer would be a betrayal of the cause. For three years, according to the common estimate, he had carried on his ministry up and down the land and now, at last, he offers himself to the nation as the promised deliverer.[1]

In keeping with this purpose, Jesus deliberately chose to fulfil the Scripture prophecy that was widely discussed by the rabbis of that day: "Behold, thy King cometh unto thee: he is just, and having salvation; lowly, and riding upon an ass, and upon a colt the foal of an ass" (Zech. 9:9).

Second, Jesus chose to enter Jerusalem as he did because he loved Jerusalem in spite of all the opposition that some of its people (especially its religious leaders) had shown him. He would give them one last opportunity to acclaim him as the Anointed of God.

Third, he was now ready to come to grips with the religious leaders. His death at their hands was inevitable. There was no better way to bring the issue to a head than to make a dramatic entrance into the city and to receive the homage of the multitudes.

The response was tremendous. In something of a frenzy,

the people plucked the branches from the trees and threw them in the road, as they customarily did in welcoming a visiting sovereign, crying: "Hosanna; Blessed is he that cometh in the name of the Lord" (v. 9). It was a fitting tribute to the coming Deliverer, but all too soon the crowd dispersed. With their lips they praised him. In their hearts they rejected him as their true Saviour.

Upon arriving in Jerusalem, Jesus went to the Temple and "looked round about upon all things" (v. 11). Since the day was far spent, he held his peace for the moment and quietly withdrew from Jerusalem to spend the night with the twelve.

II. The Withered Fig Tree (11:12–14)
(Cf. Matt. 21:18–19; Luke 21:37–38)

On the following day (Monday), as Jesus and his disciples returned to the city, he saw, in the distance, a fig tree that was in leaf. Upon approaching the tree, he discovered "nothing but leaves" (v. 13).

There has been much discussion about this incident. Did Jesus yield to a moment of petulance and impatience over so small a matter as being disappointed at not finding figs, even though it was not the season for the tree to bear fruit? The obvious explanation is that Jesus was not petulant and impatient. Rather, he saw an occasion to illustrate to the twelve the spiritual condition of the religious leaders that they would face, in the city, next day.

> In that fig tree so advantageously situated, so abundant in promise, yet fruitless, Jesus saw an emblem of Israel. He had already likened her to such a tree and warned her of the doom which would overtake her; and now He reiterates His warning.[2]

Jesus pronounced sentence on the tree: "No man eat fruit of thee hereafter for ever." God's chosen people had been weighed in the balances and found wanting.

III. Cleansing the Temple (11:15-19)
(Cf. Luke 19:45-48)

It is not surprising that Jesus became indignant at the situation that prevailed in the Temple of the Lord at Jerusalem.

In building the Temple, the Jews had made one of the few gestures of a universal outreach that is to be found in the Jewish faith of that day. It was solemnly decreed that no "heathen unbeliever" might set his foot within the sacred inner courts of the Temple, but on three sides of the Temple proper there had been built an outer court which was known as the court of the Gentiles. In this portico, the rabbis and the scribes were to teach Gentile inquirers concerning the one true God.

For the sake of the revenue they could derive from it, the Temple authorities had turned the court of the Gentiles area over to traders and money-changers, who enjoyed a profitable business. Every Jew was required to pay his Temple tax each year about the time of the Passover. This tax had to be paid in a special coinage. Visitors from remote places were obliged to exchange their money for the recognized coinage. Likewise, visitors coming from afar needed to procure the animals that were to be used by them as sacrifices during the Passover season. To meet these demands, the merchants and the money-changers had set up their stalls and their tables in the area which had been designed for teaching Gentiles the truth of God.

As a result, there was constant confusion in the Temple area, quite out of keeping with an attitude of reverence and quite contrary to the purpose for which this area had been designated. In fact, the people generally had made the court of the Gentiles a common thoroughfare.

Fearless of the consequences, Jesus began to drive out the

traders. He turned over the tables of the money-changers, and took over the Temple court, declaring, "Is it not written, My house shall be called of all nations the house of prayer? but ye have made it a den of thieves" (v. 17).

A significant thing about this episode is the effect that it had upon the scribes and Pharisees. Jesus was publicly denouncing them for allowing such a condition to exist. He was questioning both their spiritual discernment and their religious authority. In response, they must have murmured to one another, "Who does he think he is? By what authority does he set himself over us?"

From that moment, the issue between Christ and the religious leaders of Jerusalem was clearly drawn. They must get rid of Jesus or lose their place of leadership in the eyes of the people (v. 18). Jesus left the Temple to spend the night outside the city with the twelve (v. 19).

IV. A Lesson in Faith and Prayer (11:20–26)
 (Cf. Matt. 21:20–22; Luke 21:37–38)

The next day (Tuesday), as Jesus and the disciples made their way back to the city, Peter pointed to the withered fig tree, apparently with some surprise that it had already withered. Matthew points out that the disciples asked, "How did the fig tree immediately wither away?" (Matt. 21:20 ASV).

In this question, Jesus saw another opportunity to enforce a spiritual lesson. He went on to speak to his disciples about faith and prayer. It is as though he were saying to them: "Don't ask how this could happen. 'Have faith in God.' With God all things are possible. 'For verily I say unto you, That whosoever shall say unto this mountain, Be thou removed, and be thou cast into the sea; and shall not doubt in his heart, but shall believe that those things which he saith shall come to pass; he shall have whatsoever he saith'" (vv. 22–23).

The mountains of difficulty that we face time and again are no match for the power of God. The prayer of power, however, can be known only to the believer whose life is in tune with God. Effective prayer has no limits, but it does have its conditions. One of these conditions, as Jesus had previously indicated in his Sermon on the Mount, is a forgiving heart (vv. 25–26).

V. Conflict with the Religious Leaders (11:27 to 12:40)

(Cf. Matt. 21:23 to 23:39; Luke 20:1–47)

Returning to the Temple, Jesus found the religious leaders seething over the blow that he had dealt their prestige the day before. He was met by an official delegation from the Sanhedrin, the ruling council of the Jews. Already they had met and "sought how they might destroy him" (11:18).

1. *The Authority of Jesus* (11:27–33)

The religious leaders asked Jesus to state clearly by what authority he had taken charge of things in the Temple precincts. Jesus decided to let them answer their own question. They were familiar with the ministry of John the Baptist. They doubtless remembered that he had vigorously denounced them and their evil ways. So Jesus asked from whence John had received his authority. The implication is that Jesus claimed to receive his authority from the same source—directly from God.

The question left the accusers speechless. To acknowledge that John's authority came from God would have been to grant Jesus the same right to speak in God's behalf. To deny John's divine sanction would have meant stirring up the crowds against them, since John's name was still held in awe by the people. Jesus won the argument easily, but he did not win his opponents. They reasoned, all the more, that the only way to silence his opposition was to get rid of him.

2. *An Indictment of the Religious Leaders* (12:1–12)

Probably the delegation from the Sanhedrin was still standing before Jesus as he turned to the crowd and delivered what has been called the parable of the wicked husbandmen. The details of the parable were all too clear to the religious leaders.

The vineyard is Israel (cf. Isa. 5:1–7). The owner of the vineyard is God. The wicked husbandmen are the scribes, the elders, and the chief priests. The servants that were sent to the husbandmen by the owner are the prophets of Israel, some of whom had been violently abused by the religious leaders and the people of their day.

The owner's son is the promised deliverer—Jesus himself, whom the religious leaders, at that moment standing before him, had already determined to destroy. But they would not be able to destroy him, really, for Jesus went on to say that their own Scriptures foretold, "The stone which the builders rejected is become the head of the corner" (v. 10). The reference here is to Psalm 118:22.

The point of the parable is that God is still the owner of the vineyard, regardless of what the tenants may do to his Son.

This parable was directed primarily to the Jewish nation and especially to its leaders. Nevertheless, there is a timeless lesson in this story for all of us as Christians. It is that privilege invariably entails obligation. As Jesus said on another occasion: "For unto whomsoever much is given, of him shall be much required" (Luke 12:48).

3. *A Question About Tribute* (12:13–17)

The delegation from the Sanhedrin had been thoroughly defeated by Jesus in their attempt to ensnare him. Apparently they talked the matter over and decided to send to him representatives of two opposing schools with reference to the payment of poll tax to the Roman government.

The Pharisees, on the one hand, resented having to pay taxes of any kind to Rome. It was an insult to their national honor. The Herodians, on the other hand, desired to strengthen the frail grip that the House of Herod had upon political leadership and prestige. To do this they desperately needed the support of the Roman government. Hence, they were, for expediency, in favor of paying tribute to the Roman Empire.

It seemed to the religious leaders that Jesus certainly could not escape from the trap that they had thus cunningly set for him, especially in view of the lavish compliment with which they prefaced their question (v. 14). If Jesus decided against paying the tax, he would immediately find himself in trouble with the Roman authorities. If he decided in favor of paying tribute, he would antagonize the multitudes who at that time seemed to be on his side.

As always, Jesus was the master of the situation. He called for a *denarius* (penny) and asked: "Whose is this image and superscription?" (v. 16). The answer was quite obvious. The denarius bore the image and superscription of Caesar, who alone had the right to mint gold and silver coins in the Roman Empire at that time. This answer was all that Jesus needed to avoid the trap that had been set for him. Those who used the coin of the Empire must pay to Caesar whatever their earthly sovereign had the right to demand of them; no less, they must render unto God, their heavenly sovereign, whatever he demanded of them.

Jesus set forth a timeless principle that applies with equal force to our own day. As citizens, we have certain binding obligations that we simply cannot evade; it is our solemn duty to fulfil them. As servants of God, we have other obligations that are equally binding upon us.

Without diminishing in the least the necessity of fulfilling our obligations in both of these areas, it must be kept in mind that whenever these two loyalties are in irreconcilable conflict—if they ever are—then, our paramount duty is to God.

4. *Concerning the Resurrection* (12:18-27)

One would imagine that the religious leaders would at length have grown weary of trying to ensnare Jesus—so deftly did he parry their thrusts. Yet they doggedly held on for, in a very real sense, their very existence was at stake. If they were to retain their leadership, they simply could not countenance defeat at the hands of Jesus. It was not long, therefore, before another group—the Sadducees—confronted Jesus. (This is the only time that Mark mentions them in his Gospel.)

The Sadducees were few in number but they were well represented in the Sanhedrin. For the most part, they were wealthy and well-educated men. They accepted only the Pentateuch as the Scriptures. They did not believe in angels nor in spirits nor in the resurrection of the body from the grave. In fact, the Jewish historian Josephus tells us that, to the Sadducees, the spirit died with the body.

In keeping with their traditional belief, these Sadducees asked Jesus a question that was calculated to make the resurrection of the body appear ridiculous and absurd. The law of Moses decreed (Deut. 25:5) that if a widow was left childless her husband's brother should "take her to him to wife" so that the first-born child of this second union might carry on the deceased brother's family line.

The illustration the Sadducees used was quite farfetched. It is likely that they had confused the Pharisees more than once with that very illustration, but they did not confuse Jesus. He declared, first, that they did not know the Scriptures (v. 24). Their own Scriptures, if properly understood, should have removed all doubts from their minds as to the reality of the resurrection of the body.

Then, Jesus continued, they did not understand the power of God (v. 24). "God's power could accomplish the resurrection notwithstanding all real and imaginary difficulties."[3]

Again, they did not understand the nature of the future life. Earthly conditions do not any longer exist in the future life. "The entire matter of marriage, and child-birth, is applicable to the earthly life only and not to the life to come."[4]

Finally, Jesus declared that the Sadducees did not understand the nature of the character of God. He is the God of the living, not the God of the dead. A proper understanding of the character of God makes belief in the fact of life beyond the grave inevitable. (v. 27).

5. *The Question of a Scribe* (12:28–34)

One after another, the representatives of the several religious and political groups had filed before Jesus, seeking to discredit him—the chief priests, the scribes, the elders, the Pharisees, the Herodians, and the Sadducees. One after another, he had put them to rout.

All of this opposition, it would seem, had occurred in the precincts of the Temple, on Tuesday, during the Crucifixion Week. Throughout it all, there was a scribe standing in the crowd who was greatly impressed with the dexterity and the insight of Jesus (v. 28). At last, he stepped forward to put Jesus to the test. He wanted to know what was the essence of the law. Lenski remarks:

> In order to understand both the question and the answer, we should recall that the rabbis counted no less than six hundred and thirteen commandments—two hundred and forty-eight positive and three hundred and sixty-five negative. Among so many, some would, of course be less important than others and in a conflict of duties the more important would have precedence.[5]

Jesus gave the scribe a sympathetic hearing and a clear and forthright answer. He quoted a passage from the Old Testament (the Shema, Deut. 6:4–5). Until this day, this passage is the central prayer of Judaism. "It is the heart of every Jewish service. It is recited by the Jew when he believes that death is approaching." [6] In Jesus' day, this passage was the call to worship in the Temple service. The scribe found himself in total agreement with Jesus' statement. That, he surely believed.

That was not all. Jesus went on to say that there was a second commandment which was also of central importance: "Thou shalt love thy neighbour as thyself" (v. 31). With the significance of this commandment, the scribe was no less familiar. The great Jewish teacher, Hillel, had once said, "What you would not have done to yourself, do not to your neighbor; that is the whole Torah (law) and all the rest is commentary." [7]

But, for the first time, perhaps, the scribe saw the relationship of these two commandments. They belonged together. Love of God must be coupled with love for man if the laws of God are to be fulfilled. Indeed, Jesus implied that the two commandments are essentially one, as he said: "There is none other commandment greater than these" (v. 31).

We live in a day when necessity is laid upon all of us who follow Christ to heed his words to the inquiring scribe. Hatred and ill will and contempt for others do not belong in the heart of one who professes to love God, through Jesus Christ, with all of his soul and all of his mind and all of his strength.

When the scribe enthusiastically accepted the interpretation of Jesus Christ, our Lord warmly commended him saying: "Thou art not far from the kingdom of God" (v. 34). That incident put an end to the questioning.

6. *Rebuking the Scribes* (12:35–40)

Let it be noticed that Jesus judged men, not as groups but as individuals. He would not condemn a man because that man was affiliated with a group which ordinarily opposed Jesus, if the man's own attitude was right and his motives pure. Perhaps, however, it was because Jesus did not desire his fervent approval of an individual scribe to be construed by the onlookers as an approval of the scribes in general that he went on as he did.

Immediately after the inquirer had left him, Jesus began to rebuke the scribes in two connections. First, they insisted that the Messiah would be a "second David,"—an earthly potentate, a temporal king (v. 35). From the Old Testament, Jesus argued this was not the divine intent at all (v. 36). The promised Messiah would, positionally, not be David's son and successor in the temporal sense but David's Lord, and would be exalted to the right hand of God.

Jesus had still further criticism for the scribes in general. They liked to proclaim their intellectual superiority by parading in their official teachers' robes; they were haughty. Furthermore, they took pleasure in receiving the homage of the crowds as they walked through the streets; they were vain. Again, they were always looking after their own interests and seeking "the chief seats in the synagogues, and the uppermost rooms at feasts" (v. 39); they were proud. Again, they did not hesitate to extract money from the poor (widows); they were unprincipled. And finally, they prayed long prayers just to make an impression on the people; they were hypocritical.

The indictment was scathing. It would seem that Jesus deliberately invited the antagonism of the scribes; but his criticism was only the truth, and a word which they had long needed to hear.

VI. THE WIDOW'S MITE (12:41–44)
(Cf. Luke 21:1–14)

How utterly different in tone are the next recorded words of Jesus! When Jesus faced evil and corruption, he was outspoken and indignant. When he saw evidence of true piety and devotion, he was genuinely sympathetic and appreciative.

Sitting in the precincts of the Temple, he was in plain view of one of the thirteen receptacles that were placed here and there to receive the offerings of the people. He had noticed several individuals dropping in their offerings. Men of obvious means and affluence deposited sizable sums; though, indeed some such men may have given a mere pittance.

Eventually, there appeared a woman (probably in the court of the women) whose drab attire proclaimed her to be a widow. By all standards, she might very well have been excused altogether from making an offering. Yet into the box she dropped two copper coins, the combined value of which was less than one cent.

She gave least of all? Not so, said Jesus! "Verily I say unto you, This poor widow cast in more than all they that are casting into the treasury: for they all did cast in of their superfluity; but she of her want did cast in all that she had, even all her living" (vv. 43–44 ASV).

Here we have Jesus' statement as to the standard by which men should measure their gifts to the Lord. It is not, primarily, the amount of the gift that earns our Lord's approval, but the spirit of the giver and the extent to which the element of sacrifice is involved.

We know from the opening statement in chapter 13 that the disciples were about to express their admiration for the beauty of the Temple; Jesus pointed out the beauty of an act of devotion. The disciples were, no doubt, looking at the largeness of the gifts; Jesus looked at the liberality of a heart. Of course there is beauty and liberality in the large gifts of the rich when such gifts come from devoted hearts. The Master is pleased with such consecrated offerings, but it seems as if his special tenderness is felt for the cheerful giving which wells up from the overflow of grateful, adoring spirits, of whom it can be said "the abundance of their joy and their deep poverty" have "abounded unto the riches of their liberality" (2 Cor. 8:2).

Professor Hersey Davis often used to say to his seminary students: "One tenth belongeth unto God? Is that it? No. Actually, all that we are and all that we have, belong to God."

Thus, Jesus came to the close of a very busy day. All the day long he had striven with his opponents with only two bright spots to relieve the tension of the conflict—the one, an earnest inquirer; the other, a generous giver. As the day ended, Jesus left the scene of the Temple, with the twelve, terminating his last public ministry in Jerusalem. He would next return to the upper room for the last supper with his disciples and thence to Gethsemane and a night of trials, and then on to the cross.

SUGGESTIONS FOR STUDY AND DISCUSSION

1. Discuss the significance of the triumphal entry. Was it actually a triumph for Jesus? In your opinion, what was Jesus' central purpose in entering Jerusalem so dramatically at that particular time?

2. With the help of a harmony of the Gospels, outline the events of Passion Week in chronological order, as far as possible, and include the outline in your notebook.

3. In your notebook, outline the three controversies with the religious leaders in Jerusalem, giving: (1) the religious group involved in each case; (2) the basic question involved; (3) a summary of Jesus' reply.

4. Discuss the Christian standard of giving as it is revealed in the story of the widow's mite.

5. Make your outline of Mark 11:1 to 12:24 in your notebook.

---

[1] E. T. Thompson, *The Gospel According to Mark* (Richmond: John Knox Press, 1954), p. 179.

[2] David Smith, *In the Days of His Flesh* (New York: Harper & Brothers, 8th ed.), p. 395.

[3] John A. Broadus, *Commentary on the Gospel of Mark* (Philadelphia: The American Baptist Publication Society, 1905), p. 101.

[4] Richard C. H. Lenski, *Interpretation of Mark's Gospel* (Columbus: The Wartburg Press, 1934), p. 529.

[5] *Ibid.*, p. 585.

[6] Philip S. Bernstein, *What the Jews Believe* (New York: Farrar, Straus and Cudahy, Inc., 1950). Used by permission.

[7] Frederick C. Grant, *The Interpreter's Bible* (Nashville: Abingdon Press, 1951), VII, 1847.

CHAPTER 7

I. THE GREAT APOCALYPTIC DISCOURSE (13:1-37)
   1. The Destruction of the Temple (vv. 1-4)
   2. The Fearful Days Ahead (vv. 5-23)
   3. The Coming of Jesus in Power (vv. 24-30)
   4. The Second Coming of Christ (vv. 31-37)

II. THE ANOINTING AT BETHANY (14:1-9)

III. JUDAS' PATHETIC BARGAIN (14:10-11)

IV. THE LAST SUPPER (14:12-25)

V. THE PLIGHT OF THE DISCIPLES (14:26-31)

VI. JESUS' AGONY IN THE GARDEN (14:32-42)

7

FINAL HOURS WITH THE DISCIPLES

Mark 13:1 to 14:42

FOR A BRIEF PERIOD before the tragic hour of the cross, Jesus was alone with his disciples and friends. He took this opportunity to say some things that were both profound and significant. Some of these things had to do primarily with the twelve and the difficulties that would face them in the years ahead. All of his teachings during this period, however, were filled with meaning for his followers until the end of time.

I. THE GREAT APOCALYPTIC DISCOURSE (13:1–37)
(Cf. Matt. 24–25; Luke 21:5–36)

It is widely held that the great discourse as recorded in the thirteenth chapter of Mark's Gospel is one of the most difficult passages in the New Testament to understand and interpret. There are several reasons for this.

In the first place, the discourse is written in what is called apocalyptic language, that is, with the use of terms and symbols that have a hidden meaning. Because of the unsettled state of the Jewish nation at that time, it was not expedient for Jesus to set forth in bold and simple language the prediction of events that would so clearly describe its impending doom. It was for a similar reason that John used such involved symbolism in the book of Revelation. His readers would catch the significance of his statements but, if his words reached the ears of the Roman authorities, they would be at a loss to know what he was talking about. So, Jesus clothed his words in a rich symbolism that would have meaning for his disciples in that day but which are difficult to interpret today.

In the second place, Jesus deliberately intertwined his references to the destruction of the Temple with his references to things that were to follow that fateful incident, including his second coming. Throughout this passage one sentence may refer to the fall of Jerusalem while the next sentence may go on, immediately, to describe Christ's coming again at the end of the age. Again, this device was used to make his words unintelligible to those who might attempt to convict his followers of disloyalty to the authority of Rome.

In the third place, this passage must be understood in the light of the literary background of the day in which it was written. Commenting on books which reflect this background, William Barclay writes as follows:

> Between the Old and New Testaments there was a time when the Jews knew no freedom. In that time a popular literature grew up. Jesus would know it. All of the Jews would be familiar with its picture. These books are dreams and visions of what will happen when "the day of the Lord" comes and in the terrible time immediately before it. They continue to use the Old Testament imagery and to supplement it with new details but it must be noted that all these books are dreams and visions. They are poetry, not prose. They were never meant to be taken prosaically as road maps of the future and timetables of events to come.[1]

It was in this contemporary literary style that Jesus couched his message to the disciples. This explains, in part, why this passage which is so difficult for us to understand could be both meaningful and helpful to the disciples who heard it.

Finally, it should be remembered that the writers of the

Gospels were not primarily concerned with giving a connected and strictly chronological account of Jesus' teachings. This is demonstrated especially by Matthew in his Gospel. He gathers up certain happenings and certain of the teachings of Jesus according to their subject matter and not strictly in the order of their happening. It is quite possible that Mark did this sort of thing in the present passage.

While reporting the great discourse of Jesus to his disciples at the end of his earthly ministry, Mark may have included sayings that were given on other occasions, because they were of the same tenor and tone as those that Jesus uttered at this particular time. If this is actually what Mark did, then that would account for the change of theme from one paragraph to another and, in part, for the difficulty that the interpreters experience in seeking to explain the meaning of this passage. It must be remembered, however, that we have this passage as the Holy Spirit led Mark to write it, and the divine Author stands ready to reveal its truths in increasing clarity to the devout student.

1. *The Destruction of the Temple* (vv. 1–4)

As Jesus left the Temple after his long and strenuous day of conflict, the disciples gazed admiringly at the magnificent building with all of its beauty and apparent strength. They said in effect, "Look at those tremendous stones." (The historian Josephus records that some of them were sixty-five feet in length, eight feet broad, nine feet high). "What a marvellous building this is!"

To the enthusiastic remarks of the disciples, Jesus replied, possibly with genuine pathos in his voice, "Seest thou these great buildings? there shall not be left one stone upon another, that shall not be thrown down" (v. 2).

This statement was incredible. Yet, less than forty years later (A.D. 70), the marching armies of Rome, under the leadership of Titus, the son of the Emperor Vespasian, completely leveled the building and utterly destroyed the entire city of Jerusalem. As Josephus records:

> And truly the very view itself of the country was a melancholy thing, for those places which were before adorned with trees and pleasant gardens were now become a desolate country every way, and its trees were all cut down: nor could any foreigner that had formerly seen Judea and the most beautiful suburbs of the city, and now saw it as a desert, but lament and mourn sadly at so great a change.[2]

Apparently the startling prediction made by Jesus deeply disturbed the disciples, but they said nothing until they had reached the slopes of the Mount of Olives when, once again, the brilliant white facade of the Temple, overlaid lavishly with plates of gold, came into view. It was then that Peter, James, John, and Andrew drew Jesus aside and said to him: "Tell us, when shall these things be? and what shall be the sign when all these things shall be fulfilled?" (v. 4).

2. *The Fearful Days Ahead* (vv. 5–23)

Jesus then painted a very dark picture of the terrible days that lay ahead for the disciples and for all the people of Jerusalem. False deliverers would appear (v. 6). There would be wars and rumors of wars (v. 7). There would be earthquakes, famine, and unspeakable sorrows (v. 8). The Temple itself would be profaned before it was destroyed (v. 14). The only wise thing for them to do would be to flee for their lives (v. 15). Indeed, said Jesus, as he described the horrors of the days to come, "And except that the Lord had shortened those days, no flesh should be saved" (v. 20).

Just as Jesus' prediction of the destruction of Jerusalem was to be literally fulfilled, so his prophecy of suffering and disaster was historically fulfilled exactly as he foretold. The years immediately preceding the fall of Jerusalem (A.D. 66–70) were possibly the darkest days in the history of the Jew-

FINAL HOURS WITH THE DISCIPLES 105

ish nation. It has been said that they are the darkest pages in the history of any nation.

Some of the religious leaders (the disciples of Hillel) supported the Roman government, even going so far as to proclaim Vespasian the emperor their deliverer or "messiah." Others, (the disciples of Shammai), supported the revolt against Rome as it was led by John Giscala, of Galilee; Eleazer, of Idumea; and Simon ben Giorga, of Jerusalem. These leaders also posed as deliverers (messiahs) though their motivating drive was personal ambition and material gain. For four years the nation was in a seething turmoil.

The effects of this internal strife were appalling. Josephus describes the prevailing poverty and suffering in grim and graphic words:

> What was otherwise worthy of reverence was in this case despised; insomuch that children pulled the very morsels that their fathers were eating out of their mouths; and what was still more to be pitied, so did the mothers as to their infants. When they saw any house shut up, this was a signal that the people within had gotten some food. Whereupon, they broke upon the doors and ran in, and took pieces that they were eating out of their very throats.[3]

Jesus pointed out that, besides enduring the terrors of the siege of Jerusalem, his disciples would be called upon to endure persecution at the hands of the religious leaders of the day. They would be summoned before rulers and kings (as was Paul, Acts 25); they would be brought before the members of the Sanhedrin (as were Peter and John, Acts 4:6). In some cases the followers of Christ would be betrayed to the political authorities by members of their own families (v. 12).

In all of this suffering, Jesus told them, they were not to be afraid; God would give them the words to speak in the hour of their trial (v. 11). They were not to believe that

106   A STUDY OF THE GOSPEL OF MARK

these evil days were the immediate portent of their Lord's return, for, said Jesus, "And then if any man shall say to you, Lo, here is Christ; or, lo, he is there; believe him not" (v. 21).

3. *The Coming of Jesus in Power* (vv. 24–30)

At this point in his great discourse, Jesus turned to the period following the fall of Jerusalem as he said, "But in those days after that tribulation, the sun shall be darkened, and the moon shall not give her light." (v. 24).

E. J. Thompson has an interesting interpretation of the following verses (24–30). According to this interpreter, Jesus did not skip from the day of the destruction of Jerusalem to the time of his second coming. Rather, this interpreter holds, Jesus went on to describe the "era of the gospel" which lies between the fall of Jerusalem and the second coming of our Lord.

This era was something that the generation to which Jesus was speaking would certainly witness, at least in part (v. 30). During that era, which is our present age, Jesus would come in power. The new movement that he came to establish, the kingdom of God amongst men, which in that day numbered only a comparatively few believers, would become a mighty army of God which would be gathered from "the four winds, from the uttermost part of the earth to the uttermost part of heaven" (v. 27).

If the description of the natural disturbances in the earth and in the heavens, described in verses 24–25, seems to make the foregoing interpretation unlikely, it should be remembered that these verses are quite similar to the words of Peter on the day of Pentecost (quoted from the prophet Joel), which Peter interpreted figuratively to describe the advent of the Holy Spirit and the beginning of the gospel era (Acts 2:16–20). So interpreted, they seem to imply God's dramatic interference in the affairs of men and of nations through the power of the living Christ and by the work of the Holy Spirit.

4. *The Second Coming of Christ* (vv. 31–37)

In due course, and at a time that only God the Father knows (v. 32) this age will end and Jesus will come to earth again in fulfilment of the promise on the day of his ascension, "This same Jesus, which is taken up from you into heaven, shall so come in like manner as ye have seen him go into heaven" (Acts 1:11).

Though, like the man who sees the signs of summer in the budding of the fig tree (vv. 28–29), discerning souls may sense the imminence of the coming of the Lord, yet it is not within our province to know in advance the precise moment of his appearance. Our part is to be watchful and prayerful (v. 33), to be ready when the Lord shall come (v. 37). It is more than that, however. We are to be ceaselessly occupied in the work that God has given into our hands (v. 34), the work of preaching the gospel to men and women of every nation.

The late Queen Victoria was a devout Christian. On one occasion, a distinguished clergyman visited her and the conversation turned to the second coming of Christ. During the conversation, the queen is reported to have said, "I am looking for the coming of the Lord, and I do not think it impossible that I may not have to surrender my crown until I lay it down at his feet." This same expectancy, surely, should be the attitude of all of us who, as Christians, look for his appearing.

II. THE ANOINTING AT BETHANY (14:1–9)
(Cf. Matt. 26:1–13; Luke 22:1–2; John 12:2–8)

At the conclusion of the great discourse, Jesus and the disciples made their way to Bethany. At that very moment, the chief priests and scribes were assembled in the court of Caiaphas the high priest (see Matt. 26:3), plotting how they might take Jesus "by craft, and put him to death" (v. 1).

That night, or perhaps the following night, an unknown man, who is simply identified as Simon the leper, gave a supper for Jesus and his disciples and friends. Lazarus, recently raised from the dead, was a guest of honor (John 12:2) while his sisters, Martha and Mary, served the meal. While they were all reclining at the table, Mary came forward with a cruse of precious ointment and anointed the feet of Jesus, wiping them with her hair (John 12:3), and pouring the balance of the oil over his head.

This sort of thing would be quite unusual in our day but, in the day of Jesus, it was quite customary to sprinkle a few drops of sweet-smelling oil on the person of a guest. What was unusual about Mary's gracious act of love was the lavishness of her gift.

The alabaster box that Mary emptied on the feet and the head of her Master was valued at three hundred denarii. When it is remembered that a denarius was the average day's wage of a working man, the response of the disciples can well be understood. A man would have to spend a whole year's wages to buy a gift like that! It is little wonder that the onlookers murmured, "Why was this waste of the ointment made?" (v. 4).

John tells us that the murmuring was led by Judas Iscariot, who was not thinking of the poor (John 12:6). As the treasurer of the group, he was a thief and wanted to get his hands on the money that Mary's gift represented.

The response of Jesus was prophetic. Even as he sat at meat, his thoughts were on the momentous days immediately ahead of him. Perhaps the sensitive soul of Mary had sensed the impending tragedy and she deliberately anointed Jesus' body beforehand in preparation for his death. Whether she consciously meant her anointing to have that significance we cannot know, but that was the way in which Jesus interpreted it.

John A. Broadus has pointed out that, even for the poor,

Mary did far more by this act of sympathetic affection than she could have done by selling the ointment for their benefit, for that loving action "has inspired ten thousand deeds of unselfishness."[4]

III. Judas' Pathetic Bargain (14:10–11)
(Cf. Matt. 26:14–16; Luke 22:3–6)

The story of Judas Iscariot, from that moment forward, is a tragic one. Along with the other disciples, he had attended Jesus through all of the years of his earthly ministry. He had witnessed Jesus' many miracles of power and listened to his matchless teaching. Up until this moment in Mark's story, the disciples had not apparently noticed any defection in the attitude or the behavior of Judas. Instead, he had been given a place of honor in the group. He was their treasurer.

What was it that caused Judas to go directly to the chief priests in Jerusalem and to offer to deliver Jesus into their hands when an opportune moment presented itself (v. 11)? Some have said that it was his basic dishonesty that led him to make such a shameful proposition. He was crazed with the desire for money. If he could not have the three hundred denarii that Mary expended in anointing Jesus, then he would lay hold upon the thirty shekels that the chief priests would offer him for his betrayal of his Master.

Others believe that Judas did not fully realize what his betrayal of Jesus would finally accomplish. In support of this explanation, it is suggested that Judas Iscariot still held to the belief that Jesus was a temporal Messiah. He anticipated that, when Jesus was actually faced with the prospect of death, he would deliver himself by his mighty power. Then he would set up a material kingdom upon the earth and he, Judas, would continue to be the treasurer in the newly established realm.

The basic explanation for Judas' act is afforded by Luke, who declares, "Then entered Satan into Judas surnamed

110   A STUDY OF THE GOSPEL OF MARK

Iscariot" (Luke 22:3). To put it bluntly, sin was the cause of Judas' downfall. Judas had kept company with Jesus through the years but he had not allowed the spirit of Jesus to enter his soul nor the message of Jesus to strengthen his character. When the hour of fearful temptation confronted him, he was too weak to resist it.

IV. THE LAST SUPPER (14:12–25)
(Cf. Matt. 26:17–29; Luke 22:7–30; John 13:21–30)

The hour of Jesus' death was drawing near. As the day of the Passover approached, Jesus decided that he would take one last opportunity to prepare his disciples for the awful catastrophe that awaited them. So he sent two of his disciples, Peter and John, (Luke 22:8) ahead of him to make preparations for the paschal meal.

Whether Jesus had previously arranged for the use of the upper room, we do not know. Certainly, it was quite unusual, in that day, for a man to be carrying a water jar upon his head. This was a task usually assigned to the women. It is quite possible that Jesus used this unusual procedure in directing Peter and John to the appointed place because he did not want the rest of the group to know of the location in advance. If Judas had known, he might have seized the opportunity to advise the chief priests of Jesus' whereabouts.

As the group reclined around the table in the upper room, Jesus ate his last paschal meal with his beloved followers (Luke 22:15). In a real sense, it was the last Passover meal that any of his group would eat for, thereafter, the religious rite of most significance to them would no longer be the Passover of the Old Testament but the Memorial Supper of the new covenant.

It was probably towards the end of the Passover meal that Jesus announced the presence of a traitor in their midst. Apparently, the disciples had not yet suspected Judas Iscariot of disloyalty. At Jesus' words they began to look, not at one another, but each man into his own heart saying, "Is it I?" (v. 19).

In response, Jesus declared that it was, indeed, one of them, and went on to say, "The Son of man indeed goeth, as it is written of him: but woe to that man by whom the Son of man is betrayed! good were it for that man if he had never been born" (v. 21). It was God's foreordained purpose that Jesus should be crucified, but the responsibility for his betrayal lay, not with God, but with the betrayer.

It was at this point that Jesus instituted the Memorial Supper. Taking up the unleavened bread that lay before him on the table, and reaching for the cup that was on the table Jesus said: "Take eat: this is my body" (v. 22) and, "This is my blood of the new testament, which is shed for many" (v. 24).

It is quite significant that the eating of the Passover meal was immediately followed by the observance of the Memorial Supper. E. A. McDowell explains this significance as follows:

> Jesus sees himself in this meeting as bringing to a close the old sacrificial system and as founding a new covenant between God and his people. The old sacrificial system, represented in the sacrifice and the Feast of the Passover, he sees fulfilled in this new covenant. In this epochal transition from an old to a new dispensation, Jesus interprets his death as the effectuating cause, the central factor. He pictures his blood as the seal of this new covenant. As an everlasting memorial of this new covenant, he founds the new Supper of the bread and the wine, the symbols of the giving of his body and his blood to seal the covenant.[5]

As we partake of the Lord's Supper, each of us is to be consciously aware of the fact that "he died for me."

V. THE PLIGHT OF THE DISCIPLES (14:26–31)
    (Cf. Matt. 26:30–35; Luke 22:31–38; John 13:13–38)

Leaving the upper room, Jesus led his disciples to the Mount of Olives, and again he sought to prepare them for the dark hour ahead. The scandal of the cross would test their courage and their loyalty and, for the moment, they would fail him, even as the prophet Zechariah had foretold (Zech. 13:7): "I will smite the shepherd, and the sheep shall be scattered" (v. 27).

To the disciples that hour would seem like the end of the world. Let them take heart, Jesus went on to say in effect, for, in spite of all appearances to the contrary, it would not be the end of everything for "after that I am risen, I will go before you into Galilee" (v. 28). What a word of comfort! What a promise of ultimate victory! "After I am risen"! But their minds were numb. They heard his prediction of tragedy but they did not hear his promise of ultimate triumph. How like the disciples are we all! The threat of doom always gains our attention. The promise of hope so often falls upon deaf ears.

With characteristic self-confidence Peter interrupted Jesus to say: "Although all shall be offended, yet will not I" (v. 29).

The words of Jesus in response to Peter's brash statement were probably not meant as a rebuke but as a warning: "Verily I say unto thee, That this day, even in this night, before the cock crow twice, thou shalt deny me thrice" (v. 30). The Jews recognized two hours when the cock crew—one about midnight and the other toward the break of day.

It is of interest to remember that Mark probably learned a great deal about the story of Jesus from Peter. It would seem that, as Peter told Mark of this incident, the very words of Jesus still rang in his ears. How could he ever forget them? How vehemently he had denied the possibility of such a thing (v. 31)! How literally were the words of Jesus fulfilled!

VI. Jesus' Agony in the Garden (14:32–42)
(Cf. Matt. 26:36–46; Luke 22:39–46; John 18:1)

By this time Jesus and the eleven remaining disciples had reached a small enclosure containing olive trees—as the word

"Gethsemane" literally signifies. They had passed the site quite often. Its seclusion afforded Jesus a brief moment alone with the Father before the soldiers of the high priest came to arrest him.

Leaving eight of his disciples at the entrance to the garden, Jesus again took Peter, James, and John with him, just as he had done on the Mount of Transfiguration. Then, they were to witness his glory. Now, they were to witness his agony of soul as he faced the prospect of his death upon a cross.

At a certain spot, Jesus left the three disciples to keep watch for his enemies, for he was anxious not to have his communion with the Father disturbed at that critical moment. Alone in prayer and with deep emotion, Jesus dared to express to the Father the wish that he might be spared from the suffering that awaited him. Well did he know that this was impossible. For that very hour he had been sent of God. Quickly, therefore, he submitted to the inevitable as he prayed, "Nevertheless not what I will, but what thou wilt" (v. 36).

Returning to the three, Jesus found them sound asleep. The events of that night had taxed their physical strength. They were exhausted. Then, too, they did not anticipate the imminent arrest of their Lord. Jesus gently chided them, saying, "Watch ye and pray, lest ye enter into temptation" (v. 38). He was warning them not simply of that hour but of the more challenging hours that were yet to come for them. How well did he know, that, in spite of their best intentions, "The spirit truly is ready, but the flesh is weak" (v. 38).

Jesus' words went unheeded, for he returned again and yet again, and each time he found the disciples sleeping. Finally he said to them, "Sleep on now, and take your rest: it is enough, the hour is come; behold, the Son of man is betrayed into the hands of sinners" (v. 41).

For a moment, the humanity of Jesus seems to have faltered at the immensity of the load that he had been called upon to bear for the redemption of the world. But, in communion with the Father, the victory had been completely won. With grim determination, he aroused his sleeping disciples to face the worst that men could do to him saying, "Rise up, let us go; lo, he that betrayeth me is at hand" (v. 42).

We dare not intrude to analyze the sacred experience in the garden of Gethsemane. The Epistle to the Hebrews sheds some light on its mysteries.

"We see Jesus, who was made a little lower than the angels for the suffering of death, crowned with glory and honour; that he by the grace of God should taste death for every man. For it became him, for whom are all things, and by whom are all things, in bringing many sons unto glory, to make the captain of their salvation perfect through sufferings" (Heb. 2:9–10).

"Forasmuch then as the children are partakers of flesh and blood, he also himself likewise took part of the same; that through death he might destroy him that had the power of death, that is, the devil" (Heb. 2:14).

"Who in the days of his flesh, when he had offered up prayers and supplications with strong crying and tears unto him that was able to save him from death, and was heard in that he feared; though he were a Son, yet learned he obedience by the things which he suffered; and being made perfect, he became the author of eternal salvation unto all them that obey him" (Heb. 5:7–9).

SUGGESTIONS FOR STUDY AND DISCUSSION

1. In your Bible dictionary read an article on the Temple and make appropriate notes in your notebook.
2. Discuss the interpretation of Mark 13:24–30 that is given in this book. What is there to commend it? What are its weaknesses?

3. What should be a Christian's attitude toward the second coming of our Lord. Do we give this great event the attention it deserves? What errors in interpreting it need to be avoided?

4. Discuss Judas and his place among the twelve. Was he predestined to betray Jesus? Is he to be held morally accountable for the betrayal? Why did Jesus include him among the twelve?

5. Make your own outline of this section of Mark's Gospel.

---

[1] William Barclay, *Gospel of Mark, the Daily Study Bible Series* (Philadelphia: The Westminster Press, 1957), p. 318. Used by permission.

[2] Josephus, *Wars of the Jews* (Philadelphia: The John C. Winston Company), Book VI, p. 807.

[3] *Ibid.*, p. 799.

[4] John A. Broadus, *Commentary on the Gospel of Mark* (Philadelphia: The American Baptist Publication Society, 1905), p. 32.

[5] Edward A. McDowell, *Son of Man and Suffering Servant* (Nashville: Broadman Press, 1954), p. 177.

CHAPTER 8

I. THE ARREST (14:43–52)

II. THE ILLEGAL TRIAL BEFORE THE SANHEDRIN (14:53–65)

III. PETER'S DENIAL OF HIS LORD (14:66–72)

IV. THE TRIAL BEFORE PILATE (15:1–15)
   1. Jesus Faces Pilate (vv. 1–5)
   2. Jesus or Barabbas (vv. 6–15)

V. THE DEATH OF JESUS (15:16–41)
   1. Mocked by the Soldiers (vv. 16–20)
   2. Bearing His Cross (v. 21)
   3. The Place Called Calvary (vv. 22–28)
   4. The Mocking Onlookers (vv. 29–32)
   5. The Last Hours on the Cross (vv. 33–38)
   6. Some Reverent Souls (vv. 39–41)

VI. THE BURIAL OF JESUS (15:42–47)

8

THE ARREST, TRIAL, AND CRUCIFIXION OF JESUS

Mark 14:43 to 15:47

THE DARKNESS of Gethsemane was suddenly illumined with the light of flickering torches. The silence of the garden was shattered by the rattle of swords, the gruff voices of men, and the tramp of marching feet. Judas Iscariot, remembering that Jesus and his disciples had often resorted to this place to pray, had come to deliver Jesus to his enemies, escorted by a column of soldiers and several of the officers of the chief priests (see John 18:3).

I. THE ARREST (14:43–52)
  (Cf. Matt. 26:47–56; Luke 22:47–53; John 18:2–12)

In the dim light of the torches, it was difficult to distinguish any individual, so Judas had agreed in advance upon a signal. The man whom he would greet with the traditional greeting of a disciple for his master, a kiss upon the forehead, would be the man they sought (v. 44).

The disciples were very much afraid, but they loved their Master far too much to allow him to be taken without a struggle. Peter, in his usual impetuous way, drew his sword and aimed a blow at the head of one of the group of soldiers (John 18:10). He happened to be a servant of the high priest. Either because the light was bad or because his aim was poor, Peter missed his mark and struck the man's right

118 A STUDY OF THE GOSPEL OF MARK

ear. Jesus immediately saw Peter's plight. He was in danger of being struck to the ground by the Roman soldiers. This is implied in the words of Jesus as he restored the servant's ear: "For all they that take the sword shall perish with the sword" (Matt. 26:52).

Then, as if to divert attention from Peter's rash act, Jesus upbraided the band of soldiers. He had daily walked in the Temple teaching the people. Why had they not laid hold upon him then? The answer was obvious. They had come thus stealthily in the dead of the night because the chief priests were afraid of the reaction of the multitudes that thronged Jerusalem during the Passover. Jesus further saw in their surprise visit a fulfilment of prophecy (v. 49).

II. THE ILLEGAL TRIAL BEFORE THE SANHEDRIN (14:53–65)
(Cf. Matt. 26:57–68; Luke 22:54, 63–65; John 18:15–18, 24)

The soldiers led Jesus away to the court of Caiaphas, the high priest. On the way, they apparently stopped at the house of Annas, who may have lived near to the Mount of Olives (John 18:13). Annas was a former high priest who seems to have had a great deal of influence on the people of Jerusalem in that day. No doubt Caiaphas expected considerable popular opposition to the crucifixion of Jesus. He probably reasoned that it would do his cause no harm to bring the venerable Annas into the proceedings.

The trial before the Sanhedrin was irregular and illegal in every way, according to Jewish law.

> The court could not meet at night, nor could it meet at any of the great feasts. When evidence was taken, witnesses were examined separately and their evidence, to be valid, must agree in every detail. Each individual member of the Sanhedrin must give his verdict separately, beginning with the youngest and going on to the eldest. If the verdict was a verdict of death, a night must elapse before it was carried out so that the court might have a chance to change its mind and its decision towards mercy.[1]

All of these regulations were violated in the trial of Jesus. The Sanhedrin was not at all interested in administering justice. They had already cast their verdict: Jesus must die. Before they could persuade the Roman authorities to authorize his death, they had to discover some plausible charge that was not only a violation of their own religious laws but, no less, a violation of the laws of Rome.

The Sanhedrin was unsuccessful in its effort to find volunteer witnesses to substantiate the charges against Jesus (v. 55). The two witnesses who finally took the stand were evidently the hirelings of the court. Even these two could not agree in their testimony (v. 59). In all of the confusion, Jesus said nothing.

At last Caiaphas hit upon a master stroke. He had heard the common rumor that Jesus had been acclaimed the promised Messiah. If Caiaphas could get Jesus to agree to this popular acclaim, his case would be made, for the Roman government was already disturbed by the numerous revolts that had recently occurred. Rome was well aware of the persistent hope of the Jews that, some day, a mighty deliverer would arrive to free them from foreign domination. So, Caiaphas clearly put the question: Did Jesus claim to be the Messiah? (v. 61).

Up until that moment, Jesus had never made such a claim in so many words. By his triumphal entry into Jerusalem, a few days previously, he had dramatically lent his support to the claim, but the Sanhedrin needed something more specific than that. It was the purpose of Caiaphas to present Jesus with a dilemma. If he were to acknowledge the claim to messiahship, that would seal his doom. That was all the chief priests needed to achieve their murderous intentions. If he were to remain silent, the news of his silence would soon resound throughout Jerusalem, and he would be denounced as a pretender.

With quiet deliberation, Jesus frankly acknowledged the

claim, using the language of the Old Testament to state it—language with which the members of the Sanhedrin were all well acquainted (v. 62).

In a gesture of pretended anger, Caiaphas tore his clothing. The purpose of the trial had been fulfilled. They had the evidence they needed for the Roman court and for their own court. In the eyes of Rome, Jesus could be held guilty of treason. In the eyes of the Sanhedrin, he was guilty of blasphemy. It was a great hour for the Sanhedrin. Long had they waited for it. In a fit of delirium, they spat on Jesus and struck him and mockingly called on him, as a prophet, to give them a sample of his prophecies (v. 65).

III. PETER'S DENIAL OF HIS LORD (14:66-72)
(Cf. Matt. 26:69-75; Luke 22:55-62; John 18:25-27)

By the time the band of soldiers had arrived at the house of Caiaphas with Jesus, Peter had recovered from his earlier panic and had decided to go along with the group (v. 54). He was not admitted to the room where Jesus was put on trial. He remained in an outer court with the servants and the soldiers. The night was cold and they sat before an open fire. Suddenly, a servant girl began to examine Peter's face in the light of the flickering flame and to take note of his Galilean accent as he engaged in idle talk with the soldiers. "Are you not one of the followers of Jesus of Nazareth?" she eventually blurted out.

Again, fear gripped the heart of Peter, and saying in effect, "I don't know what you are talking about," he left the room and went out on the porch.

The sound of a rooster crowing in the night was a grim reminder to Peter of the words of Jesus a few hours earlier. Would his Master's words come true? Would he really deny Jesus over and over again? As if to indicate his determination to face up to any further temptation of the sort, it appears that Peter deliberately went back to join the servants and the soldiers. Once more a servant girl eyed him. As before, convinced that Peter was a follower of Jesus, she challenged him.

Peter was not as strong as he had supposed. He flatly denied this second accusation. When others around him brought a similar claim, Peter, for the third time, denied his relationship to Jesus and went on "to curse and to swear, saying, I know not this man of whom you speak" (v. 71).

There is no doubt that Peter's love for Jesus never failed; it was his courage that failed. His conduct, surely, was inexcusable but it was not unforgivable. The redeeming feature about the story is that Peter did not, for a moment, seek to justify himself. As soon as he had denied his Lord, his heart became heavy, and he burst into tears (v. 72).

IV. THE TRIAL BEFORE PILATE (15:1–15)

(Cf. Matt. 27:1–2, 11–26; Luke 22:66 to 23:35; John 18:28 to 19:16)

The Sanhedrin lost no time presenting their case to the Roman authorities. The trial at night had been an illegal and an informal one. To make it legal and formal, the Sanhedrin held a consultation at daybreak and agreed upon the formal charges that they would place against Jesus, before the Roman governor (v. 1).

1. *Jesus Faces Pilate* (vv. 1–5)

Throughout the pages of history, there are certain names that are always mentioned with contempt. Of no historical figure is this more true than of Pilate. He is the supreme example of a man who plainly saw his duty but did not have the courage to pursue it. And yet, it must be conceded that the Roman procurator of Judea had a difficult role to fill that day when Jesus stood before him.

From bitter experience, Pilate had learned to fear the national fanaticism of the Jews. It is said that when he first took the office of procurator, he was determined to rule the Jewish people with an iron hand. He was told that they would not tolerate images of any kind, nor the display of banners on which were emblazoned the insignia of the emperor of Rome.

Bent on teaching the Jews a lesson, Pilate ordered that the banners of Rome be placed on the flagstaff of his citadel in Caesarea. When the Jews objected, he addressed them publicly and threatened them, then and there, with death if they did not capitulate. In answer, the Jews fell on their faces before the Roman soldiers and "baring their necks, declared themselves ready to die rather than endure the violation of their laws." [2] In desperation, Pilate had yielded.

That incident had been a severe test of Pilate's ability to handle the explosive Jewish situation. Yet, as he faced Jesus, Pilate perhaps realized that this case would be a still greater test of his skill and diplomacy. The charge, of course, was that Jesus looked upon himself as a king. That was treason, but was it true? To know exactly how matters stood, Pilate bluntly asked: "Art thou the King of the Jews?" (v. 2).

Jesus replied, "Thou sayest it." In the Hebrew idiom that was not an evasion but a strongly affirmative answer and clearly meant, "What thou sayest is true."

The implications of the charge, however, were not true. The Jews sought to leave the impression that Jesus claimed to be an earthly sovereign, a temporal ruler, in opposition to the emperor of Rome. Doubtless, this is what Pilate construed Jesus' answer to mean until, apparently in a private conference, Jesus had an opportunity to explain the nature of his kingship more fully to Pilate (John 18:35-37).

In case Jesus' confession of kingship was not enough to convict him in Roman law, the Jews added further charges (v. 3). To Pilate's surprise, Jesus had nothing more to say in his own defense.

2. *Jesus or Barabbas?* (vv. 6-15)

In their accounts of the trial of Jesus before Pilate, both

Luke and John specifically record (Luke 23:4; John 18:38) that Pilate was fully convinced that Jesus was innocent of any crime in the sight of the Roman law. To let Jesus go free, however, would be to incur the bitter enmity of the Jewish leaders. That could very well mean political suicide for Pilate. What, then, could he do? Suddenly a novel idea occurred to him.

Apparently it was the custom of the Roman governors in Judea, in deference to Jewish sentiment, to recognize the Passover season by granting release to a notorious Jewish prisoner, allowing the people themselves to name the individual who would thus be granted clemency. In fact, it appears that at that very moment a crowd had gathered at the palace gates demanding that this annual custom be observed and that a prisoner be released.

It so happened that there was at that time a well-known insurrectionist lying in prison. His name was Barabbas. Evidently, this was the man the crowd had chosen for release on that occasion. Their request played right into Pilate's hands. He would condemn Jesus and thus satisfy the Jewish leaders, and then release him in accordance with the annual custom and thus ease his own conscience. But, under great pressure from the chief priests, the crowd would not hear of any such proposal (v. 11).

Hardly knowing what to do next, Pilate lamely asked the people, "What will ye then that I shall do unto him whom ye call the King of the Jews" (v. 12). What a question for a judge to ask the public! That was his decision, not theirs. In a wild frenzy they shouted, "Crucify him" (v. 13).

One of the saddest statements in this altogether sad story then follows: "And so Pilate, willing to content the people, released Barabbas unto them, and delivered Jesus, when he had scourged him, to be crucified" (v. 15). Matthew points out that Pilate then washed his hands of the whole affair (Matt. 27:24). Did he? Or will he be held accountable on the day of judgment for failing to take his stand for truth as he clearly saw it? Indeed, he has already been judged throughout the centuries as a man who wilfully did what was wrong because he did not have the courage to do what he knew to be right.

There is a vital lesson in this incident for all of us as Christians. The follower of Christ dare not see evil having its way and do nothing about it. Whatever the cost to us personally, we must take sides with God; we must stand up and be counted.

V. THE DEATH OF JESUS (15:16–41)
(Cf Matt 27:27–56; Luke 23:26–49; John 19:16–30)

The religious leaders had apparently won their bitter contest with Jesus. The verdict had been given. He was to die on a cross. His hour had come.

1. *Mocked by the Soldiers* (vv. 16–20)

The Roman soldiers were a rough lot, at best, but in their treatment of Jesus they were never more cruel nor less sensitive to the laws of common decency. It was not enough that the soldiers who were on guard in the Praetorium (the palace of the governor) at the time should make sport of Jesus. They sent word to the whole band or cohort, all of whom would number upward of four hundred men, and, like the soldiers of Herod Antipas before them (Luke 23:11), they laughingly robed Jesus in purple garments—the insignia of royalty—and derisively saluted him, even as they would have saluted their own emperor, shouting, "Hail, King of the Jews!" (v. 18).

For the soldiers, it was a gay moment. For those of us who read the story, it is the very essence of blasphemy, a shocking demonstration of the depravity of the human heart.

The soldiers did not stop with that. They placed a reed in the hand of Jesus to represent the sceptre that he claimed the right to carry and, to add to their merriment, they snatched it out of his hand from time to time and struck him over the head with it. Then, to make bad matters worse, they spat upon him. This was the strongest expression of contempt that the Jews knew. As a crowning act of blasphemy, they kneeled down before Jesus and assumed a posture of worship and adoration (v. 19).

The physical sufferings of Jesus on the cross were unspeakable. His emotional sufferings on the way to the cross, surely, were equally hard to bear. They were the sufferings of a broken heart, broken by this further demonstration of human sin and depravity.

2. *Bearing His Cross* (v. 21)

It was customary to require the condemned man to drag his cross throughout the city, bearing in his hand a written accusation of the crime for which he was to be executed. This heartless procession was designed to act as a deterrent to lawlessness.

As Jesus struggled under the load of his cross, he was accompanied by the two men who were to be crucified with him (Luke 23:32). Each of them was guarded by a detail of four Roman soldiers who would not spare the lash if they faltered on the way. Perhaps it was because of the terrible physical strain that Jesus had undergone during the trials of the night before that he found the weight of the cross too much for him. Perhaps it was the intense anguish of his soul that exhausted him.

Whatever the reason, it would seem that Jesus fell in the street as the procession reached the outer gate of the city. To avoid delay, the soldiers impressed a bystander into service and laid the cross upon his shoulders. All that we know about this man is that he was a native of Cyrene, in North Africa, and that he had two sons, Rufus and Alexander.

The mention of the names of these two sons by Mark

would imply that they were well known in Christian circles when the Gospel was written. It is thought that one of the sons may have been the Rufus who is mentioned in Romans 16:13. If this assumption is correct, we may assume that Simon became a believer and that he led his boys to put their trust in the Saviour whom he met under such strange circumstances.

3. *The Place Called Calvary* (vv. 22-28)

At last, Jesus and the two robbers arrived at the scene of the crucifixion. The exact site of "the place Golgotha" (v. 22), is not known. In recent years, just outside of the city of Jerusalem and to the north of it, a hill has been discovered with large caverns in the face of it so that, at a distance, it looks very much like a skull. This could very well be the place where Jesus was crucified. The Latin Vulgate translates "Golgotha" with the word *calvaria* and it is from this translation that we derive our word Calvary. Here, the soldiers prepared Jesus, and the others for their crucifixion. In the words of E. T. Thompson:

> Crucifixion was the most degrading method of death known to the Romans and one of the cruelest ever invented by man. The cross was commonly made by crossing two pieces of timber, the upright bar being, perhaps, eight or nine feet long. The hands and the feet were fastened to the upright and to the bar by ropes or nails, in Jesus' case, the latter.[3]

A society of wealthy women in Jerusalem had taken it upon themselves, as a humane service, to provide a stupefying drink for all who were crucified. This was given to the victims to lessen the pain, before the nails were driven through their hands and their feet. In the agony of his suffering, Jesus allowed the cup to be placed to his lips, but, when he had tasted it (Matt. 27:34), he refused to drink it.

Meanwhile, the four soldiers who were in charge of the

THE ARREST, TRIAL, AND CRUCIFIXION OF JESUS 127

proceedings began to claim the garments that Jesus had been wearing, "casting lots upon them, what every man should take" (v. 24).

Mark carefully notes that it was about nine o'clock in the morning (the third hour after sunrise) that Jesus was raised upon the cross (v. 25) and mentions the official accusation that was nailed to the cross, above his head: "The king of the Jews" (v. 26). It was written in three languages—Hebrew, Greek and Latin (John 19:20). It was on this charge that Jesus had been sentenced to death.

On either side of Jesus was a "robber." The word here used may equally well be translated "insurrectionist." In a sense, they were not common criminals but, rather, impulsive and misguided men who had dared to offer leadership to the Jews who were desperately anxious to throw off the shackles of Roman domination. Luke tells us that one of these insurrectionists was bitter to the end, while the other had faith enough to say to Jesus, "Remember me when thou comest into thy kingdom" (Luke 23:42). Thus, again, were the Scriptures fulfilled, "And he was numbered with the transgressors" (v. 28). The reference here is to Isaiah 53:12.

4. *The Mocking Onlookers* (vv. 29–32)

We see in the crucifixion the very heart of our Christian faith. Even as we read the story, we stand before the cross with reverent and grateful hearts, giving thanks to God that he so loved the world as to give his only begotten Son.

There was nothing of this reverence and awe in the hearts of most of those who witnessed that redemptive event. Instead, they mockingly wagged their heads in derision at this one who, as they understood it, had claimed to have the power to rebuild the magnificent Temple of Herod in three days (v. 29). Why did not he use that power to save himself from this shameful death (vv. 29–30)?

The chief priests and the scribes were no less brutal, no

128 A STUDY OF THE GOSPEL OF MARK

less irreverent. How is it, they wanted to know, that he who claimed to be able to save others could not save himself? (v. 31). Let him come down from that cross "that we may see and believe" (v. 32). The plain fact is that, even then, they would not have believed in him. He had demonstrated his power and his authority time and again without avail.

5. *The Last Hours on the Cross* (vv. 33–38)

Mark records that, from noon until three o'clock in the afternoon, darkness covered the whole land (v. 33). Then, at the ninth hour, Jesus cried, "My God, my God, why hast thou forsaken me?" The original words are given by Mark (*Eloi, Eloi, lama sabachthani*) to explain why the onlookers thought that Jesus was calling upon Elijah.

It is difficult for us to imagine that God would have withdrawn from his Son even for a moment, and especially at that terrible moment. One explanation that has been offered is that, in the moment of his death, as he bore upon himself the sins of the world, Jesus felt himself to be utterly alone. But, if this were true, then it was just for a moment, for, in his next word, the sense of God's presence is again with him as he says, "Father, into thy hands I commend my spirit" (Luke 23:46). And, crying with a loud voice, Jesus died (v. 37).

A frequent and quite plausible explanation of this cry of Jesus from the cross is that he was meditating on Psalm 22, which begins with the very words he used. In his suffering he was saying these words audibly. If this interpretation is correct, then Jesus was not expressing a complaint, for the psalm goes on to express exaltation and victory and to say at last: "They shall come, and shall declare his righteousness unto a people that shall be born, that he hath done this" (Psalm 22:31). Historically, this is precisely what has happened.

In symbolic demonstration of the work of redemption that

Jesus wrought in his death upon the cross, the curtain in the Temple that had separated the holy of holies from the holy place was split from top to bottom (v. 38).

Each year, on the day of Atonement, the high priest had raised this curtain to enter into the holy of holies, where the great stone which occupied the place of the lost ark of the covenant symbolized the presence of God. There, he made atonement for the sins of the people. In the light of Christ's death, the services of the high priest were no longer to be necessary. All who believe in Jesus may now enter "boldly unto the throne of grace, that we may obtain mercy, and find grace to help in time of need" (Heb. 4:16). Our atonement is in Christ.

> Jesus paid it all,
>   All to him I owe.
> Sin had left a crimson stain,
>   He washed it white as snow.
>
> ELVIRA M. HALL

6. *Some Reverent Souls* (vv. 39–41)

We have seen that most of the people mocked Jesus in his death. It is refreshing to find, even at the scene of the crucifixion, some reverent and believing souls. One of these was a Roman centurion (v. 39). John A. Broadus says:

> The Greek is ambiguous and may mean "a son of God." We cannot tell how much the centurion meant by the phrase. He had heard the bystanders say in their railing that Jesus claimed to be the Son of God but he would not know how much that meant. At any rate, we know that the centurion and his companions were convinced that the crucified one was not a criminal but a righteous man.[4]

Then there were the women, faithful followers of Jesus who, though not previously mentioned in Mark's account, had ministered to Jesus' needs during his great Galilean tour.

It is providential that the faithfulness of the women is mentioned in connection with the story of the cross. Throughout the history of the Christian movement, women have played a significant part in the service of Christ. Without their faithfulness and their generosity and their willingness to serve, the progress of the gospel throughout the world would have been greatly impeded.

VI. THE BURIAL OF JESUS (15:42–47)
(Cf. Matt. 27:57–66; Luke 23:55–56; John 19:31–42)

One of the witnesses to the crucifixion was a man named Joseph, of Arimathaea, who was a member of the Sanhedrin. John indicates that Joseph was a secret disciple "for fear of the Jews" (John 19:38). While he did not make a public confession of his faith in Jesus, he did object to the Sanhedrin's treatment of Jesus (Luke 23:51). When he saw Jesus die on the cross, Joseph threw all caution to the winds and boldly went to Pilate to get permission to lay the body of Jesus in a tomb that he had doubtless prepared for himself. Pilate was surprised that death had come so quickly (v. 44) but, learning from the centurion in charge of the crucifixion that Joseph's report was correct, he granted the request.

On the way back to Golgotha, Joseph bought a supply of the fine linen that was used to prepare a body for burial. The fact that he did not also procure the necessary spices would indicate that he had already talked with Nicodemus, also a member of the Sanhedrin. It was evidently agreed that Joseph would provide the tomb and the linen bandages, and that Nicodemus would provide the spices. (See John 19:39). Together they laid their Lord in a sepulchre which was hewn out of a rock, "and rolled a stone unto the door of the sepulchre" (v. 46).

Thus was Jesus buried in the new tomb of the rich man Joseph, again fulfilling the Scriptures (Isa. 53:9). The tender ministry of Joseph and Nicodemus to Jesus in the hour of his death has given their names a place of honor in the New Testament. It would seem that Nicodemus had acknowledged Jesus during his lifetime (John 7:40-52). Joseph took a brave stand at the burial of Jesus. But would it not have been much better had they but had the courage to make an unmistakable assertion of their acceptance of Jesus as their Master during his public ministry?

SUGGESTIONS FOR STUDY AND DISCUSSION

1. With the help of a harmony of the Gospels, outline the trials of Jesus in chronological order, indicating in each case (1) before whom Jesus appeared; (2) the question or questions asked; (3) the outcome.

2. Discuss the denial by Peter. Are there any extenuating circumstances? Should he have stayed away from the court of the high priest, in the light of Jesus' warning? In what way did Peter's conduct and attitude after his denial differ from that of Judas Iscariot after his betrayal?

3. For your notebook make a list of the groups around the cross and the reaction of each group to the death of Jesus.

4. Outline this section of Mark in your notebook.

---

[1] William Barclay, *Gospel of Mark, the Daily Study Bible Series* (Philadelphia: The Westminster Press, p. 368. Used by permission.

[2] David Smith, *In the Days of His Flesh* (New York: Harper & Brothers, 8th ed.), p. 478.

[3] E. T. Thompson, *The Gospel According to Mark* (Richmond: John Knox Press, 1954), p. 232. Used by permission.

[4] John A. Broadus, *Commentary on the Gospel of Mark* (Philadelphia: The American Baptist Publication Society, 1905), p. 136.

CHAPTER 9

I. ANNOUNCEMENT TO THE WOMEN AT THE TOMB (16:1-8)

II. APPEARANCES OF THE RISEN LORD (16:9-14)
   1. To Mary Magdalene (vv. 9-11)
   2. To Two Disciples (vv. 12-13)
   3. To the Eleven (v. 14)

III. THE GREAT COMMISSION (16:15-16)

IV. SIGNS OF POWER (16:17-18)

V. THE ASCENSION OF THE RISEN LORD (16:19-20)

9

THE RISEN LORD

Mark 16:1–20

DARKNESS covered the earth when Jesus died on Calvary; and darkness filled the hearts of his beloved disciples. The light of their very lives had gone out. As Jesus had foretold, they were as sheep without a shepherd (14:27). Probably they cowered for fear somewhere in the city of Jerusalem. What should they do now? Where could they go?

The story is told that, on the day that Wellington of England met Napoleon at Waterloo, arrangements were made to relay the news of the outcome of the battle from one ship to another, by semaphore, across the English Channel. A group of men stood anxiously waiting on the shores of England. Suddenly, the ship closest to the shore began to signal the message. Letter by letter, the anxious men on the mainland read the words: "Wellington defeated . . ." Then a bank of fog cut off all view of the ship. Was that all? If it was, that could mean the end of England. After some moments, moments that seemed like hours to the waiting Englishmen, the fog cleared away and the signaler began his message over again: "Wellington defeated Napoleon!"

This story is a vivid illustration of the experience of the disciples of Jesus following his death upon the cross. On Calvary, the only message that the hearts of the disciples could read was: "Christ defeated . . ." But, on the first day of the week, the resurrection morn, the whole glad message came through: "Christ defeated death!"

134 A STUDY OF THE GOSPEL OF MARK

If the central message of the gospel could be summarized in two brief sentences, they could well be these: "Christ died for our sins," and, "Now is Christ risen from the dead." The cross has long been recognized as the symbol of our Christian faith, but the empty tomb is no less significant. Paul summed up the matter when he wrote: "And if Christ be not risen, then is our preaching vain, and your faith is also vain" (1 Cor. 15:14).

By the resurrection of Jesus from the dead we mean that his body was lifted out of the tomb by the power of God and that he lives again. Someone has said that the gospel story of Jesus began with a miracle—the miracle of the virgin birth, and ended with a miracle—the miracle of his bodily resurrection. This is what the New Testament clearly teaches. This we believe!

The resurrection of Jesus, therefore, is the cornerstone of our Christian faith. To quote Paul again: "That if thou shalt confess with thy mouth the Lord Jesus, and shalt believe in thine heart that God hath raised him from the dead, thou shalt be saved" (Rom. 10:9). Not to believe in the resurrection of Jesus means not to believe in Christ as Saviour. And indeed, not to believe in the resurrection of Jesus is to have no assurance of our own resurrection from the grave.

I. ANNOUNCEMENT TO THE WOMEN AT THE TOMB (16:1–8)

(Cf. Matt. 28:1; Luke 24:1–8; John 20:1)

Early on Sunday morning following the crucifixion, some of the women who had ministered to Jesus in Galilee sadly made their way to the tomb of Joseph to anoint the body of their Master. The Jews had a way of counting days inclusively. Assuming that Jesus was crucified on Friday (and it must be remembered that the Scriptures do not specifically tell us on which day of the week our Lord was crucified) then Friday would be counted the first day; the sabbath, the second day; Sunday, the third day.

Usually the bodies of loved ones were anointed at the time of death, but there had been no opportunity for these friends of Jesus thus to honor him. Belatedly, therefore, they went forth to perform this traditional ceremony that meant so much to the Jews.

In their bereavement, the women had overlooked one very practical matter. How could they gain access to the tomb? It was the custom in those days to seal a tomb against intruders by rolling a large circular stone before the entrance. As they neared their destination, the women began to say to one another, "Who shall roll us away the stone from the door of the sepulchre?" (v. 3).

Their concern was needless for, looking up, "they saw that the stone was rolled away: for it was very great" (v. 4). Even then, the glad truth did not dawn upon their hopeless hearts, so they went in to perform their sad ritual. Then "they saw a young man sitting on the right side, clothed in a long white garment" (v. 5). They were greeted with the startling announcement: "He is risen; he is not here: behold the place where they laid him" (v. 6).

Recall that Mark probably heard much of the story of Jesus from the lips of Peter. How it must have gladdened Peter's heart to report the announcement of the angel as he said: "But go your way, tell his disciples and Peter that he goeth before you into Galilee: there shall ye see him, as he said unto you" (v. 7). The risen Lord wanted his disciples to hear the glad news, especially Peter.

Doubtless, the shame of his denial still haunted Peter. He wondered whether his Lord would ever forgive him for his inexcusable cowardice. Here was the answer. Of course he was forgiven; and Jesus would see him again in Galilee.

Good news is often as difficult to accept and to comprehend as is bad news. This was certainly the experience of the women at the tomb. They received the announcement of the angel with mixed emotions. Their hearts rejoiced at what they heard, but they were at the same time filled with fear and fled from the tomb.

II. Appearances of the Risen Lord (16:9-14)

(Cf. Luke 24:13-32, 36-43; John 20:11-25)

Readers of the Gospel of Mark who use some version other than the King James will probably notice that, at Mark 16:9, a notation is inserted. In the American Standard Version we read: "The two oldest Greek manuscripts, and some other authorities, omit from ver. 9 to the end."

Charles B. Williams, in his translation, says in a footnote: "End of Mark in two best manuscripts. Later manuscripts add vv. 9-20."

The Revised Standard Version has a similar notation and prints in italics two variant endings that appear in some of the old manuscripts.

We must face this problem frankly. What do the translators mean by this comment? The late A. T. Robertson, widely known as a New Testament scholar in his day, has this to say about the matter, in his book *Studies in Mark's Gospel*[1] (a revision of which has recently been made by Heber Peacock and is available in our Baptist Book Stores):

> There is every evidence that we have here an independent composition, a sort of early epitome of the appearances of Jesus after the order of the documents used by Luke to which he refers in his Gospel, 1:1-4. . . . It is possible that the last leaf of the autograph (the original Gospel of Mark) was lost before any copies were made of it. In the papyrus roll the last leaf would be the first to be torn off. . . . If Mark did write more of his Gospel and if copies were made of the autograph before it perished and before that leaf or leaves disappeared, then, some day we may see the true ending of Mark's Gospel.

In the light of this scholarly judgment of so conservative and competent a student of the New Testament as Dr. Robertson, we may assume that verses 9-20 were added by a later hand. This creates no real problem. All of the material covered in these verses are in full accord with the writings of the other Synoptic Gospels—Matthew and Luke—with the possible exception of verse 18 which bears a striking similarity to Luke 10:19.

1. *To Mary Magdalene* (vv. 9–11)

The several appearances of Jesus after his resurrection are a little difficult to place in chronological order. In his *Harmony of the Gospels*, Robertson lists eleven appearances in the following order (five on the first Sunday): (1) to Mary Magdalene, at the tomb; (2) to other women, in Jerusalem (Matt. 28:9–10); (3) to the two disciples on the road to Emmaus; (4) to Simon Peter, in Jerusalem (Luke 24:33–35); to the disciples (Thomas being absent) in Jerusalem (John 20:19–25); (6) to the eleven, in Jerusalem, the following Sunday (John 20:26–31); (7) to seven disciples by the Sea of Galilee (John 21); (8) to more than five hundred on a mountain in Galilee (Matt. 28:16–20); (9) to James the brother of Jesus (1 Cor. 15:7); (10) again to the disciples (Luke 24:44–49); (11) to an unknown number on Mount Olivet just prior to his ascension.

History and art have painted quite an ugly picture of Mary Magdalene. She has been identified with the sinful woman mentioned in Luke 7:37 and has been portrayed as a woman of the streets. All of this is sheer legend. All that we know about her is that she had been healed of demon possession, and, ever after, was devoted to the service of Jesus. Apparently, she outran the other two women as they tremblingly left the tomb, and found Peter and John, who returned with her.

The two disciples saw the discarded burial clothes and ran off to tell the others (John 20:5–10). Mary Magdalene remained to weep. While she wept, the angels asked her why she was so deeply troubled. In deep distress she answered them, "Because they have taken away my Lord, and I know not where they have laid him" (John 20:13).

Then Jesus appeared in the garden of the tomb and, "supposing him to be the gardener," Mary repeated the same broken-hearted lament. Tenderly he called her by name. At that, she recognized him. She would have fallen at his feet and clung to him, but he said: "Touch me not; for I am not yet ascended to my Father" (John 20:17). A more accurate translation is, "Stop clinging to me." Leaving the garden, Mary could hardly wait to break the news to the others, "as they mourned and wept" (v. 10). They were not immediately convinced. It was good news indeed but, to them, it seemed too good to be true.

2. *To Two Disciples* (vv. 12–13)

Later, on the same day (Sunday), Jesus appeared to two disciples. These are, doubtless, to be identified with the two disciples who were walking to Emmaus, which was eight miles from Jerusalem (Luke 24:13–35).

> They were not apostles. They belonged to the rank and file of the Lord's followers, and they were departing from Jerusalem in deep dejection believing that all was over. They had heard of the strange events of the morning: how Peter and John had found the Sepulchre empty, and how some of the women had seen a vision of angels who said that Jesus lived.[2]

The statement in verse 12 that Jesus appeared to the two men in "another form" is somewhat difficult to understand. Perhaps it means that his appearance was different after the resurrection from what it was before the crucifixion. This would account for the fact that Mary Magdalene did not recognize him until he spoke to her. It would also account for the fact that Thomas was not convinced that Jesus had risen from the grave when he first saw him after the resurrection, but desired to see the nail prints in his hands and feet.

Jesus' resurrection body was a transformed, glorified body, even as the resurrection bodies of all believers will be transformed and glorified. "It is sown in corruption; it is raised in incorruption: it is sown in dishonour; it is raised in glory: it is sown in weakness; it is raised in power: it is sown a natural body; it is raised a spiritual body" (1 Cor. 15:42–44).

Not recognizing Jesus at first, these two disciples fell into conversation with him and frankly confessed their disappointment in the death of "Jesus of Nazareth, which was a prophet mighty in deed and word before God and all the people" (Luke 24:19).

In answer, Jesus showed them that they had misread the Scriptures. The promised Messiah was not, in truth, to be a victorious earthly king. He was to be the Suffering Servant. Part of the work of the risen Christ, during the forty days between his resurrection and his ascension to the Father, was to correct the false concepts of the messianic hope that all of his followers seemed to continue to hold.

The two disciples on the road to Emmaus were sadly disappointed. As they saw it, God had not fulfilled his promises. Jesus therefore carefully retraced the promises of God, beginning with Moses and running through the prophets, until at last the two men were convinced. Later they gladly confessed, "Did not our heart burn within us, while he talked with us by the way, and while he opened to us the scriptures?" (Luke 24:32).

3. *To the Eleven* (v. 14)

The other Gospel writers record two separate appearances to the apostles as a group. On one occasion Jesus came to them when Thomas was absent and, perhaps to assure them of his bodily resurrection, he ate with them (Luke 24:38–43). On the other occasion Thomas was present and, after Jesus had granted Thomas (John 20:27) the same tangible proof of his resurrection that he had previously given the others (Luke 24:39), he said, "Because thou hast seen me, thou hast believed: blessed are they that have not seen, and yet have believed" (John 20:29).

It would seem that our present verse (14) may best be identified with our Lord's second appearance to the apostles as a group. They, like Thomas, had not been willing to accept the testimony of others concerning his resurrection. This was not good for, in all the years that were to follow, men and women would come to believe in him, not through tangible proof, not because of convincing logic, but because of the testimony of others—and most of all, as we now know, because of the testimony of the Scriptures.

It was perhaps in view of all of this that Jesus "upbraided them with their unbelief and hardness of heart, because they believed not them which had seen him after he was risen" (v. 14). The acceptance of Jesus Christ as the risen Lord is not a matter of intellectual understanding. It is a matter of simple faith.

There are many things about God and Christ and the Holy Spirit and the life hereafter that the most brilliant minds will never be able to grasp. Yet, even the lowliest individual who lives may come to a knowledge of God in Christ through an act of simple faith. Many scholars have sought, by long and learned treatises, to prove the truth of the resurrection. Their finespun arguments have been of no avail to the individual who does not find it in his heart to say sincerely, "Lord, I believe."

III. THE GREAT COMMISSION (16:15–16)
(Cf. Matt. 28:16–20)

The records of the resurrection appearances of Jesus in the concluding verses of the Gospel of Mark are brief summaries. No attempt is made to elaborate on any of them; and no attempt has been made to list all of his appearances in chronological order. It is possible, therefore, that there is a lapse of time between the visit with the eleven (v. 14) and the giving of the Great Commission (v. 15).

The passage (vv. 15–16) may very well be identified with the appearance of the Lord to more than five hundred on an appointed mountain in Galilee (see Robertson's *Harmony of the Gospels,* sec. 181) as recorded in Matthew 28:16–20. To place the passage in that setting would be in accord with the real purpose of the Great Commission. It was not confined to the disciples of that day. It is a commission that is given to all who follow Christ. Every believer is charged with the responsibility of proclaiming the gospel of Jesus Christ to all the world.

The day has almost passed when we hear a believer in Christ say, "I do not believe in missions." In this scientific age, when all the world has been made a neighborhood so that we are conversant with the condition of men and women on every part of the globe, no thoughtful man can bring himself to say, "What that man in a far-off continent believes is no business of mine."

We have discovered that the beliefs of other peoples is very much our business; that wrong ideas about God and wrong ideas about righteousness and wrong ideas about truth can quite easily, and quite quickly, leap across the seven seas to affect our way of believing and our way of thinking.

Today, as never before, it is clear that "the field is the world." Today, too, as never before, our function as Christians is quite clear. It is not enough to help people in the remote corners of the earth to find a "better way of life" or to improve their living conditions. We must help them to find Christ. In obedience to the command of Christ, we must "preach the gospel to every creature" (v. 15).

Basically, our mission to the world is a spiritual mission.

The world without Christ is eternally lost. He that believeth shall be saved. He that believeth not shall be condemned (v. 16).

Paul must have had the Great Commission clearly in mind when he declared: "For whosoever shall call upon the name of the Lord shall be saved. How then shall they call on him in whom they have not believed? and how shall they believe in him of whom they have not heard? and how shall they hear without a preacher?" (Rom. 10:13-14).

The statement, "He that believeth and is baptized shall be saved" (v. 16) has been the center of much controversy throughout the years. E. Y. Mullins, a noted theologian and teacher of preachers, of a generation ago, used to say to his students when confronted with such a passage as this: "A single passage of Scripture must always be interpreted in the light of the revelation of the Scriptures as a whole."

The question here is not, What does this single statement mean, by itself? but, What does the New Testament as a whole teach concerning the relationship of baptism to salvation? The answer is clear. The New Testament teaches over and over again that he who believes in Jesus Christ shall be saved. This is precisely what Jesus said to Nicodemus, who came to him inquiring the way to eternal life (John 3:16). This is what Paul said to the Philippian jailer when he earnestly asked, "What must I do to be saved?" (Acts 16:30). This, too, is what Paul wrote to the Christians at Rome when he was explaining the way of salvation (Rom. 10:9).

In each of the instances cited, salvation and baptism are not inseparably joined. Why then are salvation and baptism so coupled in this record of the Great Commission (v. 16)? The answer to this is that they belong together. In the mind of Christ, through all the ages that would follow, as men and women went out to preach the gospel, those who believed would desire to bear witness to their new life (and, indeed, to their belief in the resurrection of their Lord) through baptism. He who believes is saved.

Saving faith includes obedience. Baptism is thus the evidence of the genuineness of one's faith, for it manifests an obedient surrender to Christ. It is the normal sequence that he who is saved will, in obedience to his Lord and Saviour Jesus Christ, submit to baptism. The one is the act of saving faith. The other is the act of complete obedience.

IV. Signs of Power (16:17-18)

All of the foregoing is real and meaningful to the believer in this our day. The passage that follows, however, does not seem nearly so real nor nearly so meaningful, at first glance, to the contemporary Christian.

Jesus went on to say: "And these signs shall follow them that believe; In my name shall they cast out devils; they shall speak with new tongues; they shall take up serpents; and if they drink any deadly thing, it shall not hurt them; they shall lay hands on the sick, and they shall recover" (vv. 17-18).

There are quite a number of people who claim that this passage is to be taken literally in every generation. In some sections of the country there are professional snake handlers who persuade their congregations that God has promised to provide them with immunity from the deadly venom of rattlers. Others periodically set up their tents on the outskirts of our cities and advertise themselves as "faith healers," claiming to have the power to give sight to the blind, and healing to people with chronic, and even malignant, diseases. Others continue to speak in strange tongues. The results have been a travesty upon our Christian faith.

It would seem that some of these signs were meant specifically to apply to the church in its infancy. They were attestations to the power of God. Certainly, they were not new to the early disciples of Jesus. When Jesus sent forth the twelve, he gave them power to heal the sick and to release individuals from the domination of demons (Luke 9:1). Shortly after these words (vv. 17-18) were uttered, on the day of Pentecost, people from many different countries and of many different tongues were amazed because they heard the disciples speak in their own language and they said: "Behold, are not all these which speak Galileans? And how hear we every man in our own tongue?" (Acts 2:7-8).

W. O. Carver used to point out that it is not at all unknown for missionaries to restore demon-possessed individuals to normalcy by the preaching of the gospel.

The spiritual meaning of these words should not be overlooked. There is a very real sense in which the power of God still attends the messenger of the cross and in which the presence of God still affords guidance, sustenance, and protection to those who minister in his name.

There is an evangelist in our own day who has led thousands to Christ. Many who have heard his quiet and simple message and who have observed his gracious and unassuming manner have been prompted to ask, "Wherein lies his power?" This evangelist would be the first to answer, "If I have any power, it is from God."

It should be noticed that Matthew, in his record of the Great Commission, emphasizes the spiritual power that belongs to the servant of Christ, as he reports Jesus to have said, "Lo, I am with you alway, even unto the end of the world" (Matt. 28:20).

V. The Ascension of the Risen Lord (16:19-20)

(Cf. Luke 24:50-53; Acts 1:9-12)

Mark's story of the earthly ministry of "Jesus Christ, the Son of God" (1:1) comes to an end. In him, God had tabernacled among men. He had proclaimed the new way of life that men and women of every age will manifest as they become the children of God, by faith. He had died on the cross for the sins of the world. He had "led captivity captive" (Eph. 4:8) in his resurrection from the tomb. In the forty days since his resurrection, he had transformed the fear of his confused disciples into a glowing faith. He had commissioned those who shall believe in him throughout the centuries to preach the good news of salvation. His divinely appointed mission had been fulfilled.

Concerning the ascension, Dr. Robertson has said:

> Jesus led the disciples out of the eastern gate, past Gethsemane with its tragic memories, up the familiar slope towards Bethany, beloved Bethany. The view was sublime in every direction: the Jordan, the Dead Sea, Mt. Nebo, Jerusalem. They were looking up (Acts 1:9) and Jesus was giving them a parting blessing. A cloud swept by and he was gone. Long after the cloud disappeared the entranced disciples kept gazing into the heaven, whither Jesus had gone.[3]

It is needless to try to envision the present abode of the living Christ. The words "at the right hand of God" are best interpreted as a description of his relationship with God the Father. He is no longer the Suffering Servant. He is the exalted Christ, our living Lord, who "ever liveth to make intercession" for us (Heb. 7:25).

We may close with a further word from Dr. Robertson, who says that, as the disciples watched the risen Lord ascend into heaven:

> Their upward look was interrupted by the word of the two angels that this Jesus will so come back in like manner (Acts 1:11). He had said so himself. They now know that he is risen and believe that he will come back. . . . When he came before, they crucified him; when he comes again, he will be crowned King of Kings and Lord of Lords. Meanwhile let him rule in all our hearts. "Amen: come, Lord Jesus."

SUGGESTIONS FOR STUDY AND DISCUSSION

1. Discuss the significance of the resurrection of Jesus for our Christian faith.

2. With the aid of a harmony of the Gospels, outline the resurrection appearances of Jesus indicating: (1) the time of each appearance; (2) the place of each appearance; (3) to whom he appeared; (4) what Jesus said or did upon each appearance.

3. Discuss the Great Commission and its significance for the followers of Christ in our day.

4. List in your notebook the miraculous powers that Jesus promised to his followers. How do they apply to our own day?

---

[1] A. T. Robertson, *Studies in Mark's Gospel* (New York: Harper & Brothers, 1919), pp. 137–8.

[2] David Smith, *The Days of His Flesh* (New York: Harper & Brothers, 8th ed.), p. 511.

[3] A. T. Robertson, *Epochs in the Life of Jesus* (New York: Charles Scribners' Sons, 1928), pp. 189–190.

Questions for Review and Examination

Chapter 1

1. When did Mark write his Gospel?
2. What are some of the things we know about the life of Mark?
3. Which of the apostles influenced Mark the most?
4. Give three characteristics of Mark's Gospel.

Chapter 2

5. What is meant by the term "the gospel" as Mark uses it?
6. What was John the Baptist's central message?
7. What is the significance of the baptism of Jesus?
8. Why did Jesus go into the wilderness to be tempted?
9. Who were the first four disciples, as Mark records them?

Chapter 3

10. For what four things did the Pharisees criticize Jesus?
11. What was the attitude of Jesus' brothers and sisters toward him?
12. What four parables does Mark record in this section (4:1–34) of his Gospel?
13. Name four miracles recorded in this section of Mark's Gospel (4:35 to 5:43).

Chapter 4

14. Why did Jesus feed the five thousand?
15. What did Jesus say to the Syrophenician woman?
16. Who made the great confession as recorded in this chapter?
17. Who appeared with Jesus on the Mount of Transfiguration?

Chapter 5

18. What is the secret of true greatness?
19. What is the Christian ideal concerning marriage?
20. When may wealth be a hindrance to Christian living?
21. On how many occasions does Mark record that Jesus told his disciples of his death and resurrection?

148 A STUDY OF THE GOSPEL OF MARK

Chapter 6

22. Why did Jesus make a dramatic entry into Jerusalem?
23. What illustration did Jesus draw from the withered fig tree?
24. Why did Jesus cleanse the Temple?
25. Give three of the questions that the religious leaders put to Jesus on the day of controversy.
26. How did Jesus answer the scribe's question concerning the greatest of the commandments?
27. What lesson can we derive from the story of the widow's mite?

Chapter 7

28. Name at least three things that Jesus discussed in his great discourse (13:1-37).
29. What was the real significance of the anointing of Jesus by Mary at Bethany?
30. Give three possible reasons why Judas Iscariot betrayed Jesus.
31. Name the three disciples who went with Jesus into the garden of Gethsemane.

Chapter 8

32. Name three ways in which the trial of Jesus before the Sanhedrin was illegal and irregular.
33. What was Peter's attitude after he had denied his Lord three times?
34. Why did Pilate deliver Jesus to be crucified?
35. What did the centurion say when he saw Jesus die on the cross?
36. In whose tomb was Jesus buried?

Chapter 9

37. To whom was the first announcement of the resurrection made?
38. To whom did Jesus make his first appearance after his resurrection?
39. How many appearances of Jesus after the resurrection does Mark record?
40. Give the Great Commission as found in Mark.

Directions for the Teaching and Study of This Book for Credit

I. DIRECTIONS FOR THE TEACHER

1. Ten class periods of forty-five minutes each, or the equivalent, are required for the completion of a book for credit.

2. The teacher should request an award on the book taught.

3. The teacher shall give a written examination covering the subject matter in the textbook. The examination may take the form of assigned work to be done between the class sessions, in the class sessions, or as a final examination.

EXCEPTION: All who attend all of the class sessions; who read the book through by the close of the course; and who, in the judgment of the teacher, do the classwork satisfactorily may be exempted from taking the examination.

4. Either Sunday school or Training Union credit (*to Young People and Adults only in Training Union*) may be had for the study of this book. Application for Sunday school awards should be sent to the state Sunday school department, for Training Union awards to the state Training Union department, where forms may be secured on which to make application. These forms should be made in triplicate. Keep the last copy for the church file, and send the other two copies.

II. DIRECTIONS FOR THE STUDENT*

1. *In Classwork*

(1) The student must attend at least six of the ten forty-five minute class periods to be entitled to take the class examination.

(2) The student must certify that the textbook has been read. (In rare cases where students may find it impracticable to read the book before the completion of the classwork, the teacher may accept a promise to read the book carefully within the next two weeks. This applies only to students who do the written work.)

(3) The student must take a written examination, making a

* The student must be fifteen years of age or older to receive Sunday school credit. Training Union credit on this book is not granted to Juniors and Intermediates.

minimum grade of 70 per cent, or qualify according to *Exception* noted above.

2. *In Individual Study by Correspondence*

Those who for any reason wish to study the book without the guidance of a teacher will use one of the following methods:

(1) Write answers to the questions printed in the book, or
(2) Write a summary of each chapter or a development of the chapter outlines.

In either case the student must read the book through.

Students may find profit in studying the text together, but where awards are requested, individual papers are required. Carbon copies or duplicates in any form cannot be accepted.

All written work done by such students on books for Sunday school credit should be sent to the state Sunday school secretary. All of such work done on books for Training Union credit should be sent to the state Training Union secretary.

III. THIS BOOK GIVES CREDIT IN SECTION I OF THE SUNDAY SCHOOL TRAINING COURSE.